OUTER SPACE

OUTER SPACE

New Challenges to Law and Policy

J. E. S. FAWCETT DSC

Professor Emeritus of International Law,
University of London

CLARENDON PRESS · OXFORD
1984

Oxford University Press, Walton Street, Oxford OX2 6DP

London New York Toronto
Delhi Bombay Calcutta Madras Karachi
Kuala Lumpur Singapore Hong Kong Tokyo
Nairobi Dar es Salaam Cape Town
Melbourne Auckland

and associated companies in
Beirut Berlin Ibadan Mexico City Nicosia

Oxford is a trade mark of Oxford University Press

British Library Cataloguing in Publication Data
Fawcett, J. E. S.
Outer space: new challenges to law and policy.
1. Space law
I. Title
341.4'7   JX5810
ISBN 0-19-825398-2

Typeset by Joshua Associates, Oxford

Printed in Great Britain
at the University Press, Oxford
by David Stanford
Printer to the University

Contents

    The solar system   91
    Beyond the solar system   94
    Cosmology   96

8. STRATEGIC USES OF OUTER SPACE   106
    Weaponry   106
    Surveillance   110
    Counteraction against satellites   112

9. A GENERAL VIEW   115

    Appendix A. Principal Events   123

    Appendix B. Documents   125
    Outer Space Treaty (1967)   125
    Agreement on Activities of States on the Moon and
    other Celestial Bodies (UN General Assembly
    Resolution 34/68)   132
    Convention on International Liability for Damage
    caused by space objects (1972)   144
    Convention on Registration of Objects launched into
    Outer Space (1976)   154

    Bibliography   161

    Index   163

Part I

The Province of Mankind

Outer space is the province of all mankind. So says the Outer Space Treaty (1967),[1] adopting the principle that there are areas where common interests must be served and given priority.

It is a broad political principle, which has taken an increasing hold in the world since 1945 with the advances of technology, the growth in access to large new areas, and changes in the distribution of power, all of which have been rapid and on a large scale. The rate of decolonization after 1945 exceeded all expectations, and few then would have predicted that within a generation the number of independent countries would have trebled, and that in consequence the UN membership would be in effect universal. The growing economic interdependence of countries large and small was marked in the call by the General Assembly for a new international economic order, in the realization that

the interests of the developed countries and those of developing countries can no longer be isolated from each other, that there is a close interrelationship between the prosperity of the developed countries and the growth and development of the developing countries . . . International cooperation for development is a shared goal and common duty of all countries.

But just as there are political and economic obstacles to the establishment of a new international economic order, and challenges to the notion itself, as it is expressed by the UN, so there are similar obstacles and challenges to the securing of common interests in the uses of outer space.

Let us see how the principle of common interests has been applied in various contexts.

The Antarctica Convention (1961) declared that the

---

[1] All dates given to international instruments throughout the book are those of entry into force.

neutralization of the continent was in 'the interest of all mankind'. The common interest in resources of the deep sea-bed, recognized by the UN General Assembly, has stimulated much of the Law of the Sea Conference, and in its Convention, completed in 1982, it describes this area, far larger than the whole land area of the Earth, as 'the common heritage of mankind'; and this phrase has been used to describe the Moon and its natural resources in the Agreement governing the Activities of States on the Moon and Other Celestial Bodies, opened for signature in 1979. In the Outer Space Treaty, Article I, the exploration and use of outer space is to be carried out 'for the benefit and in the interests of all countries' and is to be 'the province of all mankind'.

While not of course denying that the common heritage of mankind and the province of all mankind are overlapping concepts, it must be observed that they differ with the contexts in which they are used, for they contain two important and distinct ideas: the 'province of mankind' has rather a jurisdictional sense, while the 'common heritage of mankind' has property overtones. The first underlines significant choices of policy, as to how far internationalization is to be carried, and as to how space operations are to be managed, whatever international regulation is adopted. The second stresses the economic interests with the particular conclusion that there should not be national appropriation of these common areas.

It may now be helpful to consider the ways in which such common interests have come to be recognized internationally and then secured.

The ideas of community and property are to be found in all human society, and surely have biological roots. Over time they manifest both conflict and fusion. In most societies the possession of land or goods is seen as a natural right of the individual, which is to be generally protected from interference by his neighbours or by the community as a whole; and as communities increased in size and structure, the authority necessary to maintain order and to meet social needs came to be vested in certain individuals, often a single sovereign. Such authority and high sovereignty were then seen as a kind of property, to be expressed in notions like eminent domain. So in turn international law attributed to States the character of legal persons, having exclusive property rights over their territories.

But the ideas of community remained. In Roman law *res communis* was distinct from *res publica*, though not always separated in practice; while in this country common land has been clearly distinguished from Crown land, as well as from land in private ownership. *Res communis* came to describe an object or area of common interest, outside the ownership of individual or State. As maritime activity grew from the end of the fifteenth century, claims were made by several countries to closed seas; but by the late eighteenth century the common interest in the freedoms of navigation and fishery had prevailed, and while coastal States were each accorded a limited territorial sea, the high seas beyond were *res communes* in international law.[2]

To speak of international law concerning the high seas, or outer space, then raises questions: in what forms is it recognized, and how is it enforced? On the first question we may distinguish common law from statute law, enacted by parliament, and international customary law from conventional law. Common law and customary law both reflect, and are formed by, common practice. This can sometimes be a new development, and may embody certain political axioms such as equality before the law and the self-determination of peoples. Customary international law may sometimes be evidenced by resolutions of the UN General Assembly, such resolutions being declaratory but not strictly formative of the law. Conventional international law is embodied in treaties, sometimes designated as international agreements or international conventions or charters, which are comparable to statutes in being formally written and binding in law, but differ in that they are in principle binding only for those States which accept and so become parties to them.

How then is the law relating to the high seas or to outer space effective? In the first place, the recognized rules and

---

[2] Hugo Grotius (1583–1645) had in his controversial work *Mare Liberum* (1608) declared that the seas could not be appropriated by individual States, and that the use of the seas by any one State must leave them free to use by others.

standards are in great part observed by States because they serve the common interest, indeed it is for that very reason that they have evolved or been adopted. While sub-rules and standards may not meet particular tests of enforceability, such as compulsory judicial control, they are in effect law because they work. There is also an evolutionary factor involved. Outside authoritarian systems—and the international system is certainly not authoritarian—community law-making rests on consent. But in parliamentary systems consent has moved to consensus with the adoption of majority rule, so that there is no right of refusal to be bound, as with treaties. Now some international assemblies, for example the UN General Assembly and the World Administrative Radio Conference of the ITU (International Telecommunication Union), are already primitive parliaments. So the ITU Radio Regulations operate throughout the world; and a certain number of UN General Assembly resolutions are at least declaratory of the law. As we shall see, its resolutions on outer space have been translated with little change into the Outer Space Treaty. Admittedly this treaty depends on consent to give its provisions the formal character of law; but the General Assembly inspired the treaty,[3] and while decades may yet have to pass before it is a law-making parliament, it is on the way.

In its Charter of Economic Rights and Duties of States,[4] the UN stresses the right of every country to benefit from advances and developments in science and technology, while at the same time man has 'a solemn responsibility to protect and improve the environment for present and future generations'. So the General Assembly:

Reaffirms its belief . . . that communication by means of satellites should be available to the nations of the world as soon as practicable on a global and non-discriminatory basis.

But, aware too of the practicalities, it

recommends that States parties to negotiations regarding international arrangements in the field of satellite communications should constantly

---

[3] The codification of the law of treaties is itself embodied in a treaty: the Vienna Convention on the Law of Treaties (1980).

[4] Resolution 3281-XXIX (12.12.1974).

bear this principle in mind, so that its ultimate realization may not be impaired.

The law of the sea, as it then stood, was doubtless an influence in the constitution of a regime for outer space, and in the adoption of UN General Assembly Resolution 1962–XVIII in 1963, which was incorporated with little change into the Outer Space Treaty (1967). Under the Continental Shelf Convention (1964), appropriation of marine resources must not result in 'any justifiable interference with fishing or the conservation of the living resources of the sea'. More generally, the High Seas Convention (1962) stated that

The high seas being open to all nations, no State may validly purport to subject any part of them to its sovereignty (Article 2).

Nevertheless, the various freedoms of navigation, fishing, laying cables, and so on, in or under the high seas

shall be exercised by all States with reasonable regard to the interests of other States in their exercise of the freedom of the high seas (Article 2).

But the Outer Space Treaty (1967) goes further in asserting a common interest, rather than a mutual recognition of national interests, and provides that:

The exploration and use of outer space, including the Moon and other celestial bodies, shall be carried out for the benefit and in the interests of all countries, irrespective of their degree of economic or scientific development, and shall be the province of all mankind.

So when we read in the Law of the Sea Convention (completed in 1982) that:

Activities in the Area [the deep seabed] shall be carried out for the benefit of mankind as a whole, irrespective of the geographical location of States, whether coastal or land-locked

we see almost a reverse influence, with an idea from the regime of outer space broadening the approach of the High Seas Convention.

Forms of internationalization

Space systems and operations serve the common interests of mankind in ways for which there can be no exclusively national substitute: in telecommunications; the remote sensing of Earth resources, both living and material; meteorology; and environment management. These services are of course already in varying degrees internationalized, being managed in part by international institutions; but space operations call, both technically and geographically, for further steps. Further internationalization may take the form of bilateral or regional agreements for co-operation. For example, in 1972 the US and USSR concluded an agreement defining the following as areas of co-operation: space meteorology and the study of the natural environment; the exploration of near-Earth space, the Moon and planets; space biology and medicine; and satellite search-and-rescue systems. Further, there was to be development of co-operation in manned space flight including 'the use of joint flights of compatible docking and rendezvous systems'. The experimental flights of Apollo and Soyuz in 1975 and the assistance to Soyuz in 1983 are examples of co-operation, though the US did not renew the agreement formally in 1981 in the context of the crisis in Poland. A regional agreement having similar objectives is the Intercosmos Convention (1977) concluded by the USSR and east European countries on co-operation in the exploration and uses of outer space.

The establishment of an international authority having general functions in the management of outer space activities, might be envisaged. It would be similar to the proposed International Seabed Authority, and would go beyond the Outer Space Treaty, which contemplated a number of parallel organizations rather than a single authority. But it is probable that we shall stay, in the internationalization of space activities, with regional and technical arrangements. It may be finally remarked that, while international agreements are the means by which such arrangements are structured and are the prime source of the law applicable to them, other sources must be taken into account: the domestic law of States engaged in space activities will be relevant, as will their economic and strategic policies; and the limitations on the use of force, now recognized as general principles of law, will also be applicable.

Recognition of space operators

How far do the international instruments distinguish between States and individuals, including private corporations, in activities in the provinces of all mankind? This must be pursued further below, but for the moment, a comparison of the Law of the Sea Conventions and the space agreements will be indicative and helpful.

The Law of the Sea Conventions have, as instruments of international law, primarily been occupied with the rights and responsibilities of States, and it is to States that most of the provisions are textually directed. However, there are references to individuals, both express and indirect, which indicate or imply rights and responsibilities for them. So in the new Convention, not yet in force, under Article 112 paragraph (1) 'All States are entitled to lay submarine cables and pipelines on the bed of the high seas beyond the continental shelf', but Article 114 requires every State to provide by law that

if persons subject to its jurisdiction, who are the owners of a submarine cable or pipeline beneath the high sea, in laying or repairing that cable or pipeline, cause a break in or injury to another cable or pipeline, they shall bear the cost of the repairs.

Again, individuals using ships may be held liable for unauthorized broadcasting, or misconduct in an exclusive economic zone.[5] Commercial production of deep sea-bed resources under licence from the proposed sea-bed Authority is prescribed in Article 151; and Annex 111 contains elaborate provisions on the granting of licences and the conduct of deep sea-bed operations by contractors: in particular, title to minerals can be obtained, and the contractor is liable for 'wrongful damage' arising out of the conduct of its operations.

The outer space instruments also tend to approach space

[5] See below for a description of an exclusive economic zone.

activities as primarily State functions, and references to individuals or private corporations are slight and indirect. Reasons for this are no doubt that the industrial and financial scale of space activities, at least in the first decades, have depended on State initiative and support; and that, as an enduring factor, a large proportion of space operations have a military use or strategic purpose. So the Outer Space Treaty places responsibility upon the State for 'national activities in outer space . . . whether such activities are carried on by governmental agencies or by non-governmental entities'; and space activities of the latter shall require 'authorisation and continuous supervision by the State concerned' (Article 6). Further, an activity or experiment planned by it or its nationals, which might interfere harmfully with space activities of other States, shall be subject to prior international consultation (Article 9 (3)). The Convention on International Liability for Damage caused by Space Objects (1972) makes the launching State absolutely liable, and that includes a State from whose territory or facility the space object is launched; so that liability or fault or negligence of an enterprise engaged in the operation under contract, with the State agency or independently, would be for determination by terms of the contract or domestic legislation. The draft Moon Agreement, Article 14 (1), adopts the principle of international responsibility for space activities in identical terms with Outer Space Treaty, Article 6; but some doubt is cast on the scope of the term 'non-governmental entities' by Article 11 (3) of the Moon Agreement, which states that neither the surface nor subsurface of the Moon, nor natural resources in place, shall become the property of 'any State, international intergovernmental or non-governmental organisation, national organisation or non-governmental entity or of any natural person'. This will be discussed further below, including the question whether 'non-governmental entity' in the Outer Space Treaty, Article 6, is to be understood as not including individuals and private corporations. Finally, the possibility of private ownership of space equipment and facilities appears to be contemplated by both Outer Space Treaty, Article 8, and the Moon Agreement, Article 12 (1). We come now to outer space as the 'common heritage of mankind', with its suggested property overtones.

Rules governing appropriation

Distinctions must be made, in areas outside national jurisdiction, between appropriation by claim of sovereignty over the area or some part of it, the appropriation of particular resources found in the area, and, in appropriation, between acquisition of ownership by the State and by some other entity.[6] On claims of sovereignty, the introduction of exclusive economic zones in outer space could be considered. In its present use, an exclusive economic zone is an area of the high seas, extending up to 200 miles from the baselines of the territorial sea, in which a coastal state may exercise sovereign rights for the purpose of exploring and exploiting, conserving and managing the natural resources, and also jurisdiction for certain purposes. Proposed in an early stage of the UN Law of the Sea Conference, it became rapidly and extensively adopted in practice—an example of customary law developing in advance of treaty application.

Under the Outer Space Treaty, Article 6, outer space, including the Moon and other celestial bodies, cannot be nationally appropriated by claim of sovereignty, by means of use or occupation, or in any other way; and the Moon Agreement, Article 11 (3), specifies some of the means which cannot lead to appropriation:

The placement of personnel, space vehicles, equipment, facilities, stations and installations on or below the surface of the Moon, including structures connected with its surface or subsurface, shall not create a right of ownership over the surface or subsurface of the Moon or any areas thereof. The foregoing provisions are without prejudice to the international regime referred to in paragraph 5 of this article.

But what is obviously of greater practical interest is the appropriation of natural resources found on the Moon and other bodies. It is probable that for the foreseeable future, Mars, and perhaps its two satellites—with the perhaps warning names of Deimos and Phobos, Terror and Rout

---

[6] See generally D. S. Myers, ' "Common interest" and "Non-appropriation" in Outer Space', *International Relations* (May 1977), 529.

—will be the only accessible sources of usable substances, other than the Moon.

It may be said that, in principle, just as the high seas are declared to be open to all States, and traditionally the States have access to the seas' resources, the resources in outer space and on celestial bodies are open to all. Access to, and use of, such resources, including possible appropriation, must then necessarily be subject to international regulation. If the distinction proposed above between acquisition of sovereignty and of resources is sound, the Outer Space Treaty, Article 2, see Appendix 1, is concerned only with claims of sovereignty, and not with the appropriation of particular resources, except perhaps the orbital positions of Earth satellites, to be discussed later.

We may then see what the draft Moon Agreement has to say.[7] It makes extensive provision for the internationalization of the Moon, and other bodies in the solar system, but it does not resolve the problems of appropriation of resources. Article 11 (1) and (2) state that:

The Moon and its natural resources are the common heritage of mankind, which finds its expression in the provisions of this Agreement, and in particular in paragraph 5 of this Article.
The Moon is not subject to national appropriation by any claim of sovereignty, by means of use or occupation, or by any other means.

And under paragraph (5):

States parties to this Agreement hereby undertake to establish an international regime, including appropriate procedures, to govern the exploitation of the natural resources of the Moon, as such exploitation is about to become feasible. This provision shall be implemented in accordance with Article 18 of this Agreement.

Article 18 calls for a review of the Agreement by the UN General Assembly ten years from the entry into force of the Agreement, and for a review conference after five years to implement in particular Article 11 (1) and (5)—a parliamentary function. The US Space Industrialization Act (1978)

---

[7] The text of the Agreement was adopted by the UN General Assembly on 5.12.1979. For studies of the background and substantive provisions of the Moon Agreement, see S. Maureen Williams, 'International Law before and after the Moon Agreement', *International Relations* (Nov. 1981), 1168; and Bin Cheng, 'The Moon Treaty', *Current Legal Problems* (1980), 213.

recognizes the possibility of processing minerals, and even product manufacture, in space stations.

The functions of the international regime are similar to those prescribed for the deep sea-bed—the Area under the Law of the Sea Convention beyond national control—and are stated in Article 11 (7) to be:

(a) The orderly and safe development of the natural resources of the moon;
(b) The rational management of these resources;
(c) The expansion of opportunities in the use of these resources;
(d) An equitable sharing by all States Parties in the benefits derived from these resources, whereby the interests and needs of those countries which have contributed either directly or indirectly to the exploration of the moon, shall be given special consideration.

But the Agreement fails to make clear the character of appropriation of the resources of the Moon, or how far it may be taken, at least prior to the review contemplated in Article 18. While it might be said that Article 11 (1) and (2) exclude any form of national appropriation which constitutes sovereignty or any claim to it, other provisions of the Agreement allow some appropriation, at least indirectly. So Article 11 (3) states:

Neither the surface nor the subsurface of the Moon nor any part thereof or natural resources in place, shall become the property of any State, international, intergovernmental or non-governmental organisation, national organisation or non-governmental entity or of any natural person.

The natural resources are qualified by the words 'in place'; and the language of the paragraph as a whole indicates that its purpose is to prohibit the creation of any proprietary rights *in situ* by some form of occupancy. For stations, installations, and structures set up on the surface or in the subsoil shall not, as the paragraph later states, confer ownership of the area covered by them.

The use of mineral resources is dealt with in Article 6 (2) which is directed at scientific investigation, and provides that:

In carrying out scientific investigation and in furtherance of the provisions of this Agreement, the States parties shall have the right to collect and remove from the Moon samples of its mineral and other substances. Such minerals shall remain at the disposal of those States parties that caused them to be collected and may be used by them for scientific purposes. States parties shall have regard to the desirability of making a portion of such samples available to other interested States parties and the international scientific community for scientific investigation. States parties may in the course of scientific investigations also use mineral and other substances of the Moon in quantities appropriate for the support of their missions.

These provisions, read together, suggest the following construction. Mineral resources may plainly be removed from the Moon for purposes of scientific investigation, and their remaining at the disposal of the collecting State entails ownership of them, subject however to the requirement that they be used for scientific purposes. Mineral resources may also be displaced and used on the Moon in support, perhaps as an energy source, of scientific missions. In both cases, mineral resources are appropriated. But two question are left open: who acquires ownership of mineral resources removed for other than scientific purposes, the State or some other entity? And does the orderly and safe development, and national management, of these resources and the equitable distribution of benefits from them, under the international regime envisaged in Article 11 (5 and 7), call for more than international regulation, or for the exclusion of ownership of the resources for those who collected them? The principle that 'The ownership of space vehicles, equipment, facilities, stations and installations shall not be affected by their presence on the Moon' (Article 12 (1)), suggests that ownership of mineral resources displaced on, or removed from, the Moon may be established extraterritorially under the internal law of the State involved.

Strategic aspects

The Outer Space Treaty has not resolved the conflict between the common interests of mankind, and the expression of national fears and ambitions in what is seen as self-defence. According to an official government statement to the US Senate in May 1980:

Space systems provide critical strategic and tactical support to military forces and political leaders in the areas of attack, warning, surveillance, communications, intelligence and meteorology.

Article 4 of the Treaty does not exclude the use of outer space for such critical strategic and tactical support. The text is significant:

States Parties to the Treaty undertake not to place in orbit around the Earth any objects carrying nuclear weapons or any other kinds of weapons of mass destruction, instal such weapons on celestial bodies, or station such weapons in outer space in any other manner.

The Moon and other celestial bodies shall be used by all States Parties to the Treaty exclusively for peaceful purposes. The establishment of military bases, installations and fortifications, the testing of any type of weapons, and the conduct of military manœuvres on celestial bodies shall be forbidden.

The use of military personnel for scientific research or for any other peaceful purposes shall not be prohibited. The use of any equipment or facility necessary for peaceful exploration of the Moon and other celestial bodies shall also not be prohibited.

In the first place, this is the only part of the Treaty where a substantive distinction is made between outer space and celestial bodies. In particular, there is no provision that outer space shall be used exclusively for peaceful purposes. Further, even if the Moon and other celestial bodies must be used only for peaceful purposes, the phrase is ambiguous. Is the development of weapons that might be used in self-defence a peaceful purpose; and, if not, why are military personnel allowed to engage in scientific research, for that engagement would have at least an objective of defence, if not of prior attack?

To conclude—access to outer space and celestial bodies, and the use of this access, are indeed symbolic of the dramatic and unpredicted changes in the world over the last forty years. They remind us of the words of James Anthony Froude, observing the end of the fifteenth century:

for indeed a change was coming over the World, the meaning and direction of which is still hidden from us, the change from era to era.

So in the long view, the changes across the world since 1945 —rapid but enduring, disorganizing and productive—may be seen as making the beginning of a new era, in which mankind must learn to live in new provinces.

Space frontiers

Three kinds of frontier will be considered here: the lowest level of outer space in relation to the surface of the Earth; possible limits on space travel; and outer space as a power frontier.

The volume of space around the Earth has not been defined in terms of altitudes by any international agreement. There is a rule of customary international law, expressed in the ICAO (International Civil Aviation Organization) Convention (1947), Article 1, that: 'every State has complete and exclusive sovereignty over the airspace above its territory'. But no upper limit has been set either in State practice, or in that Convention, and it remains a matter of speculation, though both physical and functional criteria have been recommended.

The atmosphere, being similar in structure from ground level up to an altitude of about 100 km, could be described at least up to that level as airspace; and since the atmosphere, though progressively disintegrated, continues up to an altitude of around 400 km, even this higher level might be claimed as airspace. However, it is functional criteria that have influenced State practice at least up to the commencement of space operations in 1957. Before then the highest altitude reached by any conventional aircraft was about 20 km, and most aircraft were operating at no more than half that altitude. The interest of countries in their airspace being largely concerned with its usability for aviation, there was no pressure or need to introduce a higher limit for airspace; even if territorial airspace were to have been formally given an altitude limit of about 50 km, the level at which aerodynamic life becomes insufficient, this would have had little practical significance.

Space operations complicated the picture, for a new frontier had appeared. At what altitude does outer space begin? No lower limit of outer space was set in the Outer Space Treaty and the issue was left on the agenda of COPUOS (Committee for the Peaceful Uses of Outer Space). The Nuclear Test Ban Treaty (1963), Article I (a), does not refer to airspace but prohibits nuclear explosions 'in the atmosphere beyond its limits, including outer space; or under water, including territorial waters or high seas'. But it is not indicated what kind of limits are envisaged here, or whether, as the use of the word 'including' in both clauses suggests, there is a zone beyond the atmosphere, which is not yet outer space. Unless physical limits are determined for either airspace or atmosphere, no lower level for outer space beyond them can be set in physical terms. It may be observed that, in French, outer space is *espace extra-atmosphérique*.

A functional approach, though adopted to a great extent in practice, also has its dubieties. It might be said that, as airspace may be defined as that part of the atmosphere in which aerodynamic lift can keep aircraft in flight, so outer space begins at the altitude at which satellites can be maintained in orbit around the Earth, becoming literally spacecraft. But this altitude, about 120 km, would leave a zone which would be neither outer space nor airspace. It might also be said that Earth satellites, in their gravitational link with the Earth and even their orbital function, are still essentially terrestrial objects and that consequently outer space should be seen as beginning, in relation to the Earth, beyond the orbit of the most distant Earth satellites. Geosynchronous satellites, also called geostationary satellites, are at present the most distant, orbiting the Earth at an altitude of 35,400 km;[8] and eight equatorial countries, subscribing to the Bogotá Declaration (1976), claim that the segments of orbit of geostationary satellites above their territories are not in outer space but are an integral part of the territory below, a claim we shall consider later. In the various solutions which have been proposed for these space frontier problems no consensus has yet emerged among governments, and given that space activities have progressed and expanded for a quarter of a century without it, it may well be that the national limits of either airspace or outer space are not of primary interest or concern.

More romantic are the hopes of space travel. Space

[8] A geosynchronous satellite rotates around the centre of the Earth at approximately the same speed as the Earth itself, and is geostationary in that rotating with the Earth, it remains at a relatively fixed point in the sky above a given point on the surface of the Earth. Such satellites must, to achieve this, be placed in a near-equatorial orbit and at the distance indicated.

exploration has inspired a mythology, in which it is assumed that the potential range of spacecraft is unlimited, and that man can and will have contact with civilizations among the stars, leading, of course, to 'star wars'. Given the many millions of stars, similar in age and structure to the Sun, in our galaxy, and the vast number of similar galaxies so far observed, the statistical probability must be high of there being many other planets, associated with Sun-like stars, where life is nurtured and developed, often more primitive and often more advanced than on Earth. But distances make travel between Earth and such planets impracticable for spacecraft given the energy demand, and for human beings, or similar beings, impossible, given the length of time required.[9] It took Voyager 2 about four years to reach the neighbourhood of Saturn; and, outside the solar system, there have been observed two stars, very similar to the Sun and perhaps having planets around them, but at inaccessible distances.

It seems then that, for the foreseeable future, the outer solar system will remain the frontier of controlled space travel. But a dangerous development concerning outer space is to have made it a new power frontier. Writing soon after the Second World War, the Australian historian H. Duncan Hall pointed to the division of the world into two power blocs and the consequent emergence of a frontier between them—a power frontier:

The international frontier consists of the major areas, in which the major interests, activities and forces of the Great Powers—and in varying degrees of the smaller powers—meet, overlap and conflict.[10]

The subdivisions of the power frontier make many areas of conflict; both sides have for most of the time an interest in the stabilization of the frontier, but security through stabilization of 'an area of the international frontier requires forces not formulas'.[11] Outer space has become an area of conflict in the power frontier between the US and the USSR for 'the cutting edge of military competition between the

[9] See Box 1 (in ch. 2) for spacecraft velocities.
[10] 'Zones of the International Frontier', *Geographical Review XXXVIII* (1945), 615.
[11] Ibid. 624.

United States and the Soviet Union involves the use of outer space for warlike purposes'.[12] Stabilization of the frontier in outer space is all the more difficult because of outer space's geographical scale and the unprecedented rapidity of instalment in it of military devices, to be described later.

We turn now to some general aspects of space operations as they are being conducted: the functions of spacecraft and the character and status of their operators.

[12] Julie Dahlitz, 'Arms Control in Outer Space', *World Today* (April, 1982), 154.

2

Uses of Outer Space

Functions of spacecraft

The uses of outer space are illustrated by the types and functions of spacecraft, and these are summarily described in the US National Aeronautics and Space Act (1958), as amended in 1974:

S-102(c) The aeronautical and space activities of the United States shall be conducted so as to contribute materially to one or more of the following objectives:

(1) the expansion of human knowledge of phenomena in the atmosphere and space;

(2) the improvement of the usefulness, performance, speed, safety, and efficiency of aeronautical and space vehicles;

(3) the development and operation of vehicles capable of carrying instruments, equipment, supplies and living organisms through space;

(4) the establishment of long-range studies of the potential benefits to be gained from, the opportunities for, and the problems involved in, the utilization of aeronautical and space activities for peaceful and scientific purposes.

The pursuit of such objectives as these has led to the creation in the countries operating in outer space of two main types of spacecraft: Earth satellites and spacecraft travelling beyond Earth orbit. Earth satellites are placed mostly in circular or near-circular orbit,[1] and at altitudes determined by the orbital position and period, which are in turn chosen according to the capacity and functioning of the satellite, and the corresponding costs.

[1] The Molniya (USSR) series are in elliptical orbits at altitudes ranging from 500 to 40,000 km; many of the Cosmos series are in low-altitude elliptical orbits.

Box 1

All spacecraft have so far been launched by rockets, generating high-pressure exhaust gas from solid or liquid fuel, and remain under the direction of, or in communication with, ground stations.

Thrust. Rockets are governed by Newton's third law of motion that 'to every action there is always opposed an equal reaction'. Expressed in weight, the rocket thrust must at launch exceed the combined weight of rocket, fuel, and spacecraft, so that the initial acceleration overcomes gravity. But since the weight of fuels at present used represents 90–5 per cent of the total weight of the rocket, the mass of fuel is the major element. The ratio of thrust to the consumption of fuel is called the specific impulse of the rocket and is, in effect, the length of time in seconds for which 1 kg of propellant will generate 1 kg of thrust. The average impulse of conventional fuels is around 350–450 seconds. Nuclear fuels could attain 800 seconds or more. There are at present no international regulations governing nuclear-powered satellites; no safety requirements, for example.

Velocity. The minimum velocity which a spacecraft must attain in order to counter the gravitational pull of the Earth, and thus not fall back, but remain in orbit or go beyond, is 7.9 km/s or about 18,000 m.p.h.; and for full efficiency the launching rocket must enable it to attain that velocity rapidly. However, once in orbit the spacecraft is under a balance of forces, that of gravity being reduced, and its velocity will be less; geosynchronous satellites travel in orbit at about 7,000 m.p.h. It is possible then for propellants other than the initial launching fuel to be used effectively for travel in Earth orbit or beyond. So in a plasma, or stream of ions, the collection of electrified particles is of low density and small thrust, but the particles can be accelerated to very high speeds with effective thrust in a virtual vacuum. Such rockets can then form the second or later stages of a spacecraft propellant system, so that the problem of fuel weight is resolved. A photon rocket, still a fantasy, might approach the velocity of light.

Orbits. Geosynchronous orbits are used by communication satellites, including those of transmission of radio and TV, and their periods of revolution around the centre of the Earth range from 1,420 to 1,460 minutes. All other orbits in use, being elliptical, can vary widely in their altitude above the Earth, and in their corresponding period of revolution. Orbits are selected according to the function of the spacecraft though the problems of mutual interference are constantly present between orbits or between satellites in the same orbit.

Orbital movements of typical satellites

Approximate period of revolution around Earth (hrs)	Altitude of orbit (km)	Passages over some point on Earth (per day)
24	35,870	Geostationary
12	20,240	1
8	13,940	2
6	10,390	3
3	4,190	7

Earth satellites serve as means of telecommunication, including radio and TV broadcasting, data distribution, guidance for air and sea navigation, and agricultural methods, and provide atmospheric surveys[2] and meteorological reports. As instruments of Earth surveys they carry out what is called remote sensing, which includes surveys over large portions of the Earth of, for example, mineral resources, the location of fish stocks, the distribution of forests and other vegetation, and desertification. Satellites are also used for strategic surveillance, and may be vehicles for the carriage of weapons.

European telecommunication systems favour land-lines, the size of Western Europe reducing the advantages of satellites, which are most useful for transmission over great distances. The development of fibre-optic cables, superior in a number of respects to the conventional copper cables, is also advancing the case of land-lines. By contrast, in the United States the use of satellites is being steadily expanded by a number of enterprises: for example, Satellite Business Systems, partly owned by IBM, is setting up Earth receiving stations throughout the United States, the first satellite being capable of handling 840 million bits of data per second; the American Telephone and Telegraph Company, which operates most of the telephone services in the US, has been authorized to launch three Telstar satellites. Another example of the geographical range of Earth satellites is their use in linking university buildings, and consequently unifying courses, on five islands in the West Indies: Jamaica, Trinidad, Barbados, St Lucia and Dominica.

The development of the space shuttle has made possible the construction and operation of space stations; the possible assembly of prefabricated modules and the docking of space-shuttles with the stations point to the stations becoming of great and radical use. Space shuttles are already designed to carry space tugs, which are placed in low orbit and may be telecontrolled to carry payloads to stations in higher orbit. It is not hard then to foresee space stations becoming

---

[2] The Global Atmospheric Research Programme (GARP) is run jointly by ICSU (International Council of Scientific Unions) and WMO (World Meteorological Organization).

manufacturing centres, processing materials extracted from
the Moon; and they may even be made temporary or permanent human settlements, given the size to which stations
may over time be constructed in the relatively weak gravitational fields. More immediate is the possibility of geostationary satellites being constructed in order to convert
solar radiation into electric power for consumption on
Earth. The frontiers of astronomical observation have been,
and continue to be, radically extended by satellites, both in
terms of optical observation and the detection of gamma
rays, X-rays, and infra-red radiation. Recording and analysis
of radiation from the Sun have led to an understanding of the
physical processes in its atmosphere, and their terrestrial
effects. Satellite observations are notably and steadily increasing our knowledge of stellar processes, but are also
helping to identify the structure of distant galaxies, and
quasars, and so broaden concepts of the character and origin
of the universe. Spacecraft which move beyond the gravitational control of the Earth, are mainly space probes,
engaged in exploration and research. Exploration of the
solar system by spacecraft includes detailed observation
of the Sun, and surveys of the planets with landings on the
Moon, Mars, and Venus. These surveys comprise studies of
the atmospheres of, for example, Venus, Mars, and Jupiter,
and of the geological structures of the Moon and other
planets, leading to greater understanding of the formation
and age of the solar system. A small piece of rock, picked
up from the surface of the Moon by an astronaut in 1969,
was found by chemical analysis to be about 4.6 billion years
old, and this is now generally believed to be the age of the
solar system.

State responsibility for space activities

This can arise in a number of ways. In the first place, there is
the general obligation to share equitably with other countries
the resources and facilities of outer space. So the Outer Space
Treaty (1967) Article 1 (2) lays down the principle that
outer space shall be 'free for exploration and use by all
States' without any discrimination. But this cannot be limited

Box 2

Spacecraft are given many names or acronyms, sometimes describing their function or destination. Examples are (ESA is the
European Space Agency):

Communications

Intelsat I–VI

US   Early Bird
     Satcom
     (geosynchronous)

USSR Molniya
      Statsionar
      (geosynchronous)

ESA ECS (European
     Communications
     Satellite)

Strategic Surveillance

US   VELA
     IMEWS (Integrated
     Missile Early Warning
     System)
     Navstar
     (navigational)

Solar System Space Probes

US   Apollo (Moon)
     Viking (Mars)
     Pioneer (Jupiter)
     Voyager (Saturn)

USSR Lunik (Moon)
      Mars (Mars)
      Venera (Venus)

Remote Sensing

US   ERTS
     Landsat

ESA ERS (Earth Resources
     Satellite)

Meteorology

ESA Marecs A, B

USSR Meteor

Space Station and Shuttles

US   Skylab–Columbia

USSR Soyuz–Salyut

ESA Spacelab

The Cosmos series, numbered
now to over 1,000 of the
USSR, have a multitude of
functions including remote
sensing, aiding air and sea
navigation, strategic surveillance, and carrying out biological experiments (Vostok type
carries small animals, insects,
plants).

to what may be regarded as State operations in a strict sense.
On the contrary, the space activities of non-governmental
entities are not only a State responsibility, but require
authorization under the domestic law and continuing super-
visions. Article 6 provides that:

States parties to the Treaty shall bear international responsibility for national activities in outer space, including the Moon and other celestial bodies, whether such activities are carried on by governmental agencies or by non-governmental entities, and for assuring that national activities are carried out in conformity with the provisions set forth in the present treaty. The activities of non-governmental entities in outer space, including the Moon and other celestial bodies, shall require authorization and continuing supervision by the State concerned.

No distinction is made here between the State as employer or entrepreneur or owner, in whole or part, of an outer space enterprise, and the State as the ultimate national authority. The Convention on International Liability for Damage caused by Space Objects, which entered into force in September 1972, is for all its elaboration, even less clear on this critical issue. Under it:

A launching State shall be absolutely liable to pay compensation for damage caused by its space object on the surface of the Earth or to aircraft in flight. (Article II.)

In the event of damage being caused elsewhere than on the surface of the Earth to a space object of one launching State, or to persons or property on board such a space object, by a space object of another launching State, the latter shall be liable only if the damage is due to its fault or the fault of persons for whom it is responsible. (Article III.)

A 'Launching State' is defined in the same way as in Outer Space Treaty, Article 7, as a State which 'launches or procures the launching of a space object' or 'from whose territory or facility a space object is launched' (Article I (c)). A number of possibilities arise, given the distinctions between launching and procuring a launch, and between the territory and the facility from which the object is launched. A State is the launching State, liable for damage under Article II, if

(i)   it launches a space object from its territory, using its own facility; or

(ii) it launches it from the territory of another State, by arrangement with it, and using its own facility or a local facility; or

(iii) arranges for the launch of a space object in its own territory by another State or 'non-governmental entity'; or

(iv) provides a launching facility for another State for use in the territory of that State.

These conditions are also to be inferred from Article I (c) of the Convention. Damage includes 'impairment of health'; and liability of the launching State for damage caused on 'the surface of the Earth', or to aircraft in flight, is absolute, unless the launching State can show that the damage 'resulted either wholly or partially from gross negligence or from an act or omission done with intent to cause damage on the part of a claimant State or of natural or juridical persons it represents' (Article VI (1))—but these provisions do not apply to materials of a launching State.

Claims for compensation for damage are to be made initially through diplomatic channels; failing settlement, a Claims Commission shall be established at the request of either party. The guiding provisions for handling disputes are elaborate at all stages. There is no restriction on the use of nuclear-powered satellites, the only provision being that 'If the damage caused by a space object presents a large-scale danger to human life or seriously interferes with the living conditions of the population or the functioning of vital centres', special and rapid assistance shall be considered by the States in the Convention (Article XXI). The USSR placed Cosmos 954 in orbit in September 1977 carrying a nuclear reactor working on enriched uranium. In January 1978 it disintegrated, and debris entered Canadian airspace and was deposited in Alberta, Saskatchewan, and the North-West Territories. It was the first incident resulting in a convention claim. A plutonium-powered naval navigation satellite, launched by the US in April 1964, had failed to reach Earth orbit, and had disintegrated over Madagascar, but it was accepted that there was no danger of radiation reaching ground level.[3] Cosmos 954 was served by a reactor, containing up to 100 lbs of U^{235}, and two fragments with radiation traces were found at the end of that January. The USSR requested the return of all the debris recovered in Canada, but Canada made payment of at least the costs of recovery a condition of return. This condition was consistent with Article 5 (5) of the Convention on Rescue of Astronauts and Return of Space Objects, which came into force in September 1968, which makes the launching State liable for the costs of recovery and return of space objects or their fragments. No evidence of damage or injury from radiation from the

---

[3] Described in US memorandum to COPUOS (July 1978).

remains of Cosmos 954 was found, but the potential danger was plain; and Canada called on the legal subcommittee of COPUOS to prepare a new convention dealing with nuclear-powered spacecraft. A settlement of all claims arising from the fall of Cosmos 954 was finally reached in April 1981, when the USSR agreed to pay Canada the sum of three million dollars.[4]

With luck such accidents will be rare, and in practice settlement by diplomatic exchange is the most probable outcome, not least perhaps because of the legal ambiguities in the Convention. For all its legalisms, it does not answer some essential questions. Space operations may be planned and conducted by many operators, usually in collaboration; by established government departments, or a public agency created for the purpose, or by private entrepreneurs, acting perhaps under industrial or service contracts with State agencies, and the State may have an equity shareholding in such enterprises. The Convention does not, in implementing the broad terms of Outer Space Treaty, Article 6, explain at all the actual extent of State responsibility in such complex practices, or the means of its determination. 'Space object' in Article II could mean one owned by the State, or directly operated by the State, or any space object of which it is the launching State and which it therefore has under its jurisdiction and control. Again, in Article III, without further explanation there can be no difference as regards the State, between 'its fault' and 'the fault of persons for whom it is responsible'.

It may be asked whether *the rule of registration*, which has been applied to space objects, treating them as similar in status to ships and aircraft, resolves the first ambiguity. The Outer Space Treaty, Article 8, provides that:

A State party to the treaty on whose registry an object launched into outer space is carried shall retain jurisdiction and control over such object, and over any personnel thereof, while in outer space or on a celestial body.

---

[4] See XVIII *International Legal Materials* (1979), 899, and XX (1981). Between 1968 and 1979, fourteen terrestrial impacts of spacecraft were reported to the United Nations.

Further the ownership of such an object is stated to be not affected or qualified in any way by its location.

In developing the principle of registration for space objects, the Convention on Registration of Objects launched into Outer Space, which came into force in September 1976, does not determine the relation between a State and 'its' space objects. The obligation to register space objects falls on the launching State, defined in the same terms as in the Liability Convention. It would be reasonable to conclude that the category of 'its' space objects necessarily includes those registered with the State; but the question whether inclusion is limited to them remains open. The Convention in fact is concerned with the uses and procedures of registration, and has nothing to add to the Outer Space Treaty about the ownership of, or responsibility for space objects. So the only provision for international collaboration is in the tracking and identification of a space object where it has caused damage or may be of a 'hazardous or deleterious nature' and a State affected has not found the registered information sufficient to identify the object (Article VI). Further, where there is a joint operation between two or more launching States, they shall 'jointly determine which one of them shall register the object', bearing in mind 'Outer Space Treaty, Article 8, but without prejudice to appropriate agreements on jurisdiction and control over the space object and its crew' (Article II-2).

It may be replied to all these queries, that these international Conventions are only concerned with the *international* responsibilities of States for space operations; but this is to ignore the fact that the domestic law as regards, for example, ownership, agency insurance, and nationality would often have to be taken into account in international disputes, particularly as claims for compensation for damage may be brought 'in the courts or administrative tribunals' of a launching State (Liability Convention, Article XI (2)).

A further complication is presented by the recognition of *the role of international organizations* in space activities. The Outer Space Treaty, Article 6, states that:

When activities are carried on in outer space, involving the Moon and other celestial bodies, by an international organization, responsibility for compliance with this Treaty shall be borne by the international organization and by the States parties to the Treaty participating in the organization.

This statement must be read as a policy directive rather than a rule of law, for two reasons. Not all international organizations are recognized as separate legal persons, capable of assuming international responsibilities; and also, responsibilities cannot be imposed upon an organization, which is so capable, by an external treaty, unless it assents to this treaty —this is implied in Article 13. The Outer Space Treaty is limited to States, and both the Liability Convention and the Registration Convention expressly exclude international organizations from ratification or accession. However, both the Conventions provide in similar terms for the participation of international organizations. So Article XXII (1) of the Liability Convention provides that

In this Convention, with the exception of Articles 24 to 27, references to States shall be deemed to apply to any international inter-governmental organization, which conducts space activities, if the organization declares its acceptance of the rights and obligations provided for in this Convention, and if a majority of the States members of the organization are States Parties to this Convention and to the (Outer Space Treaty).

Intelsat (International Telecommunications Satellite Consortium), which succeeded an interim institution as a permanent organization in 1973, was declared in the definitive International Telecommunication Satellite Organization Agreement to possess legal personality, in both international and municipal law, and to be the owner of the Intelsat space segment.[5] Its liability for damage would then, if the reasoning above concerning Outer Space Treaty, Article 6, is correct, depend on its acceptance of the Liability Convention. Further, under Article XXII (3) its members would, if parties to the Liability Convention, be jointly and severally liable. This covers any prescribed space operation resulting in damage to others, wherever that damage is incurred, and

[5] Articles IV and V (a). See Delbert D. Smith, *Communication via Satellite* (Sijthoff, 1970), pp. 151 ff., for a description of Intelsat operations.

so corresponds to the broad scale of international liability expressed in Outer Space Treaty, Article 7. The statement quoted goes on to say that:

> The State also bears international responsibility for all acts committed by its officials or organs, which are delictual according to international law, regardless of whether the official organ has acted within the limits of its competency or has exceeded those limits.

These statements make the important distinction between the imputability to States of liability for action, or failure to act, and the characterization of either as a ground of legal liability. But the statements contemplate only the conduct of State agents; and liability under Article II for damage caused by a registered space object will extend to the State of registration, even though the space operation has been carried out by one or more private enterprises, or by another State. That this liability should extend also to the case where a State simply provides a launching facility to another State, for employment in the territory of the latter, is affirmed by the fact that they are both 'launching States' under the Liability Convention, Article V of which provides that:

1. Whenever two or more States jointly launch a space object, they shall be jointly and severally liable for any damage caused.
3. A State from whose territory or facility a space object is launched shall be regarded as a participant in the joint launching.

Under Article III, liability for damage caused to a space object elsewhere than on the surface of the Earth—though in fact delictual in a country's airspace, or beyond, or in outer space, under Outer Space Treaty, Article 7—is limited to where the damage is due to fault.

Another problem is the prevention of *intrusion on satellite communications*. A conference in Brussels in 1974 adopted a Convention on Distribution of Programme-carrying Signals by Satellite.[6] Sponsored by Unesco and WIPO (World Intellectual Property Organization) the Convention entered into force in August 1979. The prime purpose was to prevent the poaching of satellite signals for redistribution. A signal is defined in the Convention as 'an electronically-generated carrier capable of transmitting programmes', and a programme

---

[6] See text in XIII *International Legal Materials* (1974), 1446.

as 'a body of live or recorded material consisting of images
or sounds or both, embodied in signals emitted for ultimate
distribution' (Article 1). The Convention then requires the
taking of 'adequate measures to prevent the distribution
on or from its territory of any programme-carrying signal
by any distributor for whom the signal, emitted to or
passing through the satellite, is not intended' (Article 2).
The main object is to prevent unauthorized rebroadcasting,
which would infringe the rights of broadcasters, performers,
and owners of copyright, since broadcasting fees are normally
related to the presentation of particular works in a specified
region. The list of programmes protected is limited by a
number of exceptions; short excerpts from a programme,
consisting of reports of current events, and 'informatory
quotations', compatible with fair practice, may be redistri-
buted (Article 4 (i) and (ii)). Further, developing countries
are not required to take measures preventing redistribution
of satellite programmes, if it is 'solely for the purpose of
teaching, including teaching in the framework of adult
education, or scientific research' (Article 4 (iii)). And in a
Conference report it was stated that

this Convention will not be applicable to the poaching of satellite
transmissions used to transmit energy [electricity] from a solar
powered satellite to an Earth receiving antenna . . . (or) to transmissions
of scientific or technical data, military intelligence, private communications and other material presently transmitted via satellite for special-
ised use.

It may be then asked whether *humanitarian and environmental protection* have become more general forms of State
responsibility in space operations. The need for assistance
from, and sometimes rescue by, individuals in spacecraft
was recognized after the Voskhod and Gemini operations in
the mid-1960s; and in 1965 an international convention was
hurriedly drafted, coming into force in December 1968.[7] The
ITU Convention, in its revised form in 1967, has provided that:

the international telecommunications services must give absolute
priority to all telecommunications concerning safety of life at sea, on
land, in the air or in outer space (Article 39).

[7] Bin Cheng, 'The 1968 Astronauts Agreement or how not to make a treaty',
Yearbook of World Affairs (1969), 185.

Surprisingly the Rescue and Return Agreement (1968) does not expressly extend the application of this principle to outer space. More than once there is reference to the high seas or 'any other place not within the jurisdiction of a State'; and the provision concerning the return of space objects speaks of those that have fallen *on the Earth*, that is on the territory of a contracting party, or on the high seas, or 'in any other place not within the jurisdiction of a State' (Article 5 (1)). Apart from areas of Antarctica, and the high seas, there are no significant surface territories outside State jurisdiction; but it is not necessary to extend the scope of the phrase beyond the Earth, since the Moon Agreement provides that:

States parties shall adopt all practicable measures to safeguard the life and health of persons on the Moon . . . shall offer shelter in their stations, installations, vehicles and other facilities to persons in distress on the Moon (Article 10).

Further, any person on the Moon shall be regarded as an astronaut under both Outer Space Treaty, Article 5 (all possible assistance to be given in case of accident, distress or emergency), and the Rescue and Return Agreement. Some problems that remain to be resolved in application of the Agreement are whether the obligatory language of Article 4 on repatriation of astronauts to the launching State precludes a right to grant asylum; and whether a State in whose territory a space object falls, may make the return of it or its parts conditional on payment of compensation for any damage it has caused.

Environmental protection is curiously limited in the Outer Space Treaty. Article 9 requires that the exploration of outer space, including the Moon and other celestial bodies, shall avoid their 'harmful contamination'; and necessary measures must be taken for this purpose, and also in order to prevent adverse changes in the environment of the Earth resulting from 'the introduction of extraterrestrial matter'. The Moon Agreement goes a little further than the Outer Space Treaty in providing that

In exploring and using the Moon (and other bodies in the solar system), States parties shall take measures to prevent the disruption of the existing balance of its environment, whether by introducing adverse changes in that environment by its harmful contamination through the introduction of extra-terrestrial matter or otherwise,

and in requiring that the UN Secretary General be notified of the measures taken under this paragraph, and also 'in advance of all placements by them [States parties] of radio-active materials on the Moon and of the purposes of such placements' (Article 7 (2)). Further, it calls for 'orderly and safe development of the natural resources of the Moon' (Article 11 (7)).

But environmental protection is wider in having two distinct elements: the preservation of the environment by the avoidance of pollution and other harmful effects of building, transport, and so on; and the conservation of natural resources, by the avoidance of waste and unnecessary usage of resources. The second will be considered below with regard to the radio spectrum and the use of satellite tests.

Space activities may cause pollution on the Earth or other bodies in ways not yet adequately controlled, such as through rocket exhausts, the fragmentation of nuclear vehicles, and the disposal of radioactive waste. Space-shuttle rockets, equipped with solid fuel, can emit about 150 tonnes of alumina particles (AL_2O_3) in launching the shuttle, and these particles are spread through the upper troposphere and into the stratosphere; a dust layer of around 1,000 tonnes of aluminium could develop in the lower stratosphere, and the average ice-nuclei concentrations there be increased two-fold.[8]

Projects which are otherwise useful may cause pollution, such as the abortive US West Ford project in 1961. Initially called Needles, this was a passive system of telecommunications to be based on hundreds of millions of copper needles placed in orbit to act as reflectors. Overtaken in telecommunications by active satellite systems, it had been objected to as an environmental obstacle, at least to astronomical observation. Again, it is envisaged that the space-shuttle system may be used to dispose of radioactive waste from the earth in outer space, if distributed at a sufficient altitude in

---

[8] It is estimated that sixty launches of a space-shuttle in a year could reduce the ozone layer by 9.5 per cent, still however below the annual reduction caused by natural and other man-made causes, but perhaps a warning.

outer space, it would be no doubt harmless, but the hazards of transit could not be ignored. It is indeed accidents, leading to the fragmentation of nuclear-powered space vehicles, that can threaten the environment.

Both the US and the USSR have been operating nuclear-powered satellites, and there are more than twenty at present in orbit. The majority of the US satellites use a generator, in which the natural decay of U^{238} generates thermal energy, which is converted into 70 watts of electric power. This relatively low power is sufficient only for astronomical infra-red and other spectral scanning. USSR satellites, using nuclear power, have reactors in which the fission of uranium generates far higher power, of the order of 10 kilowatts, making radar scanning possible, used particularly in ocean surveys. There have been a number of accidents to nuclear-powered satellites. It is estimated that Cosmos 954 left about half a tonne of uranium and a hundred-weight of plutonium in orbit around the Earth, and another nuclear-powered satellite in the Cosmos series fell in the Pacific after launch in April 1973. A US Navy nuclear-powered satellite broke up over Madagascar in 1968 and in 1979 Apollo 13 fell in the Pacific, its nuclear battery sinking to the sea-bed. Whether a derelict satellite carrying nuclear fuel can be a hazard is uncertain, but in due course the derelict may be retrievable by space tugs.

Surprisingly the Liability for Damage Convention does not refer to the use of nuclear power in spacecraft, but it does define damage as 'loss of life, personal injury, or other impairment of health' or 'loss of or damage to property', and so the injurious effects of radiation would be covered. The Convention on the Liability of Operators of Nuclear Ships, concluded in May 1962, has some guide-lines in its definitions of nuclear ships and nuclear damage. A nuclear ship is 'any ship equipped with a nuclear power plant' (Article 1-1); and nuclear damage is 'loss of life or personal injury and loss of or damage to property' resulting from the 'radio-active properties or a combination of radio-active properties with toxic, explosive, or other hazardous properties of nuclear fuel' (Article 1-7). The Convention imposes absolute liability for such damage on the operator of a nuclear ship (Article 2).

In this area of accident and damage, the needs and demands of insurance also pose problems and even obstacles for space activities. Fire claims, based on insurance taken out for satellite operations, are known or have been made and met since 1957. How far policies are to cover faulty construction of launchers or spacecraft, or mistakes in handling by the operators, is a leading question. The magnitude of claims that may be brought is illustrated by the failure of the Ariane launcher in September 1982. Carrying two satellites that had cost around $58m. and with launching costs of $30m. it fell into the Atlantic a few minutes after launch from Kourou in French Guiana. It had been insured for only $20m. for its flight.

Discussion of environmental protection has been limited here to the provisions of the various outer space treaties, and so some other guiding principles must be mentioned.

First, it can be said that there is now a generally accepted international duty to avoid transfrontier pollution of the atmosphere: in short, the right to exploit natural resources carries with it a responsibility to avoid causing harm. So the UN Conference on the Human Environment, held in Stockholm in June 1972, set down a number of principles. Principle 21 says:

States have, in accordance with the Charter of the United Nations, and the principles of international law, the sovereign right to exploit their own resources pursuant to their own environmental policies, and the responsibilities to ensure that activities within their jurisdiction or control do not cause damage to the environment of other States or of areas beyond the limits of national jurisdiction.

We have here a statement, which given its purpose, reasoning, and authority, may, on the lines described earlier, be said to be declaratory of the law. Further, the second clause in the declaration is wider in scope than the first, and can be clearly extended to outer space activities which cause pollution in the upper atmosphere of outer space. Secondly, the absolute liability of a launching state to pay compensation for damage caused by its space object[9] is paralleled by adoption of a polluter-pays principle by the OECD:[10]

The principle to be used for allocating costs of pollution prevention and control measures to encourage rational use of scarce environmental

[9] Liability for Damage Convention, Article 2.
[10] Recommendation on Guiding Principles concerning Environmental Policies

resources . . . means that the polluter should bear the expenses of carrying the above-mentioned measures.

Again we have a principle that can be said to have the force of law.

(May 1972). Text in B. Ruster and B. Simma (eds.), *International Pollution of the Environment* (Oceana Publications, 1975), vol. 1, p. 116.

3

Space Operators

The principal operators in outer space are private entrepreneurs, governmental agencies, and international agencies;
and it is necessary to see their respective forms and working
relationships.

Outer space activities are essentially transnational, not
only in their execution, and to a great extent their preparation, but above all in the benefits and dangers that can flow
from them. There is then a common interest, spread around
the world, in the exploration and uses of outer space, though
along with the need and demand for extended co-operation
there is both competition in the scientific development and
industrial use of space technology, and conflict expressed
in the military exploitation of outer space.

The role of private enterprise

Private entrepreneurs are normally incorporated as companies, which are treated as nationals, and subject to the law,
of the countries where they are established and registered.
But the structure of private enterprise is complicated in a
number of ways: a corporate body may be created by statute,
which makes it subject to certain directives and restrictions
seen to serve the public interest, or it may be, through State
shareholding, made subject to a degree of governmental
control. However, the notions of private sector and private
companies may be said to comprise those enterprises which
are essentially independent of government in their policy and
management, and whose objectives are primarily commercial.
Again companies have branches or subsidiaries in their own
and other countries, and there can be controversy over the
range of jurisdiction over them. So a parent company and its
subsidiary in another country are each subject to the law and

jurisdiction of the country in which it has been incorporated; but can the government or legislature of the country of the parent company give what are in effect directives to the subsidiary, when those directives could be contrary to the law or practice of the country in which the subsidiary is located? Companies also often form consortia, the consortium being for some purposes the effective operator, or they engage in joint ventures and further problems concerning jurisdiction can arise.

The distribution of what are in effect public functions in outer space between the private sector of industry, separate public agencies, and established government departments, varies with the policy needs and constitutional framework of different countries. Ministers of defence, foreign affairs, communications, industry, and so on, will always have some part to play in the formation of policy and the administration of space activities, which are essentially public in purpose and range; and distinct public agencies may be established as the principal operators. In the private sector, where the involvement in space operations is largely commercial, enterprises may specialize in the production of space facilities, such as the building of satellites and launchers, or may manufacture particular instruments or equipment as a part of wider industrial production.

But, while a broad distinction may be made between space activities having a commercial interest, and those designed as a public service, it is not possible to draw lines too sharply between the functions of the private and public sectors. Many enterprises and agencies have in fact a dual role, performing a public service but also free to engage in commercial operations. Further, while on the one hand, commercial enterprises may depend on the public agencies, for example for the hiring of launchers or the leasing of communication channels, on the other, public agencies will often depend on the private sector at least for the supply of technology and equipment, obtained through commercial contracts.

Notable enterprises are Space Services Inc. and Satellite Business Systems in the United States, British Aerospace in the United Kingdom, and OTRAG (Orbit Transport und Raketen) in the Federal Republic of Germany. Satellite

Business Systems is a tripartite enterprise of IBM, Comsat, and Aetna Life Insurance, and is setting up a network of receiving stations on office roof-tops throughout the United States, in order to provide a business information service through satellites. A number of companies have also been authorized by the Federal Communication Commission to provide mixed satellite services, and are regarded as 'common carriers'.

There is much collaboration through consortia and joint ventures. British Telecom International is in partnership with Satellite Business Systems on part of the business information service; and on the home front, British Telecom, British Aerospace, and GEC–Marconi have formed a joint enterprise, called UNISAT, to launch a communications satellite in 1986, named Halley to mark the appearance of his comet in that year. The satellite will have two TV channels and also channels for commercial communications. Plessey has entered a joint venture with Scientific Atlanta, a US corporation, and a company is to be set up in England for the development of cable networks to distribute satellite broadcasts and this reflects the growing competition between cable transmission and satellite broadcasting, as it becomes progressively direct.

Examples may be given of satellite communication corporations which are established by legislation, and these range from public agencies to semi-commercial enterprises. The USSR Maritime Satellite Communication Association is described as having all-Union functions and legal personality; and, the title 'Association' being equivalent to society or company, it appears to be a separate public agency rather than part of any government department.[1]

Telsat Canada, a corporation established by the Canadian Federal Parliament as a national system, commenced operations in September 1969.[2] The statute provides that:

The objects of the company are to establish satellite telecommunications systems, providing on a commercial basis telecommunications services between locations in Canada

---

[1] For its statute see XX *International Legal Materials* (1981), 1365.
[2] Described by C. M. Dalfen in *Stanford Journal of International Studies* (June 1970), 84.

and the shares in the company are to be issued:

in such proportions among (i) Her Majesty in right of Canada; (ii) approved telecommunications common carriers; and (iii) persons who fulfill the statutory conditions, as the Board of Directors, with the approval of the Governor in Council may determine.

An interesting restriction is that the corporation is expressly forbidden to enter into amalgamation arrangements.[3]

The US Congress enacted the Communication Satellites Corporation Act in 1962, in which the broad objective is declared and the international function stressed:

a commercial communications satellite system is to be established, in conjunction and in cooperation with other countries, as expeditiously as practicable, as part of an improved global network, to be responsive to world-wide communications needs so as to contribute to peace and understanding.

Comsat was authorized by S.305 of the Act to:

(1) plan, initiate, construct, own, manage and operate itself or in conjunction with foreign governments or business entities a commercial communications satellite system;[4]
(2) furnish, for hire, channels of communication to United States communications common carriers and to other authorised entities, foreign and domestic; and
(3) own, and operate, satellite terminal stations when licensed by the (Federal Communications) Commission.

Comsat was then a US corporation, created by statute and governed by US law. It was also required, in rather imprecise terms, to submit to Presidential supervision, and to seek advice from the Department of State, given the international range of its functions.[5]

Perhaps the best-known public agency is NASA (National Aeronautics and Space Administration) in the US, which works closely with established departments such as Defense, Health Education and Welfare, and Commerce. The last has a division, entitled the National Environment Satellite Service, and the transfer to it from NASA of the management of Landsat-D is contemplated.

[3] It may be asked whether these extend to consortia or joint ventures.
[4] An Office of Industrial Applications has been established at the Marshall Space Flight Center to develop joint ventures.
[5] See Delbert D. Smith, *Communication via Satellite* (Sijthoff, 1976), p. 80, particularly for the move to commercialization.

Attitudes and policy towards the role of private enterprise in space activities naturally vary, and on the international level it is interesting to compare the Outer Space Treaty with provisions contained in the Law of the Sea Convention. The Outer Space Treaty places the exploration and uses of outer space in the hands of States. So States remain responsible for all space activities carried on by their nationals, whether the operators are governmental agencies or 'non-governmental entities'; the activities of the latter require authorization and continuing supervision by the State (Article VI (1) and (2)). 'Non-governmental entities' are not defined, but it must be assumed that they include private companies; and the forms of authorization and supervision are not specified.

The principle that activities of private enterprise must be authorized by some form of State licence, even if they may be undertaken in areas which are outside national jurisdiction, is expressed in recent legislation on deep sea-bed mining. Persons subject to US jurisdiction are prohibited from mining the deep sea-bed without a licence.[6] Such persons are:

(a) any individual who is a citizen of the United States; or
(b) any corporation or other entity organised or existing under the laws of the United States; or
(c) any corporation . . . or other entity . . . if the controlling interest in such entity is held by an individual or entity described . . . in (a) or (b) (S.4 (15)).

But a licence for deep sea-bed mining may be granted to such persons not only by federal authority, but also by a 'reciprocating State'. This is defined as a foreign State, which under its own law regulates such mining with adequate measures for the protection of the environment, the conservation of resources, and the safety of life and property at sea, and with effective enforcement provisions.

We have then an interesting development. While deep sea-bed mining may be seen as an exercise of the freedom of

[6] US Public Law 96—283, Deep Seabed Hard Minerals Act (1981). The Federal Republic of Germany has introduced similar legislation: Interim Regulation of Deep Sea Mining (1978), enacted in anticipation of the new Law of the Sea Convention. Both statutes are analysed by David D. Caron, 'Deep sea-bed Mining: A Comparative Study of US and West German Legislation', *Marine Policy* (Jan. 1981), 4.

the seas, and is in any case outside national jurisdiction, it is coming to be nationally controlled on the basis of principles that have been acquiring international recognition; the sharing and conservation of natural resources, as conditions governing the grant and use of mining licences. The principle of sharing is recognized in the Law of the Sea Convention which requires each coastal State to make payments and contributions to the International Sea-Bed Authority in respect of exploitation of its continental shelf beyond 200 nautical miles, unless it is a developing State which is a net importer of mineral resources. The Authority is to distribute these payments and contributions to States parties to the Convention on the basis of 'equitable sharing criteria'. The protection of the marine environment, the conservation of the living resources of the seas, and the best uses of its resources for the 'benefit of mankind' are also sought.

As has already been shown, the Outer Space Treaty, despite similarities of language, falls short of these objectives. In particular, it does not prescribe any conditions for the authorization of private enterprise activities in outer space, though it brings them indirectly under State supervision. It is at least now recognized that in order to make space operations effective, regulated working arrangements between private enterprise and public agencies are necessary. The US Office of Technology, in a report in 1982, observed that:

A great part of the success of the European and Japanese (space) programs results from their institutional arrangements, within which private and public sectors can work well together.

Further, in a statement in 1982 on US space policy President Reagan, while making no specific proposals for the transfer of any part of the civilian space-shuttle service to private enterprise, as sought by Space Services Inc. and other, called for 'a climate conducive to expanded private sector investment and involvement in space activities'. Substantial cuts in the NASA budget may be in part a creation of such a climate; a reduction of $367m. was called for from October 1981, and further cuts up to $1bn. were envisaged over the next two years. Abandonment of Voyager 2, at present due to go past Uranus (1986) and Neptune (1989), is considered. Proposals have also been made in the US Congress for some combination of NASA and private enterprise projects, though much must depend on the balance of contribution and control.

There is, in fact, a high level of collaboration in space activities between the private sector and public agencies, and within the private sector itself. Another group of space operators—the most vital—are those who control space operations and their results in ground stations, and those who from time to time voyage in spacecraft. The work of the first will come naturally into account in the contexts of particular space activities but the second call for some special remarks.

Man in space—a picture that is being drawn slowly in practice, but occurs often in prophetic fantasy, in which human settlements in space are taken for granted; even the social order of *Homo spatialis* is discussed.[7] It may then be worth looking at some of the difficulties that have to be overcome in travelling and living in outer space.

In 1961, astronauts from both the US and USSR went into Earth orbit for the first time. The US conducted a series of manned flights in Gemini spacecraft in 1965-6, and eleven flights in Apollo from 1968 to 1972. The duration of flights was not longer than about 15 days; but in 1973 astronauts spent about 30, 60, and 84 days in orbit in three Skylab operations. There were no further manned flights until the Space Shuttle in 1981 and Challenger in 1983. The USSR has, in contrast, while organizing fewer manned flights than the US from 1961 to 1973, embarked on almost continuous operations since then, in Soyuz or in combined docking operations of Soyuz and Salyut, the orbiting space station. At least seven flights have had durations of 75 days or more, with the maximum duration being 185 days. Much has been learnt about the difficulties of manned space flights and their practical solutions. The effects of high acceleration and of weightlessness in conditions of zero gravity can be tolerated though the latter may cause space sickness; and temperature

[7] George S. Robinson, 'Space Law as Reflection of Transnational Values', IV *Annals of Air and Space Law* (1979), 636.

can be controlled, particularly the overheating of the sunlit side of the spacecraft. But radiation in the Van Allen belts, in cosmic rays, and in high-energy particles in occasional solar flares, can be a constant hazard, and exposure must be prevented or limited by metallic shielding or the creation of magnetic fields in the spacecraft. Again the skin of the spacecraft is vulnerable against meteroids or dust particles. The requirement of a reduced weight-load for effective orbiting restricts the volume of space for occupancy of what is a sealed container like a submarine, and also the quantity of materials that may be carried, particularly of food and for air-conditioning. It may be that the development of hydroponics,[8] or of systems for making edible food from the activity of bacteria, will resolve part of the second problem; and solar cells could supply needed electricity. But it seems that it will be a long time before space travel can be much extended in time or numbers of travellers.

Residence on the Moon or Mars is still a more remote possibility. Spacesuits, not least for protection from radiation, and self-supporting breathing apparatus, would be permanent requirements for individuals, and fairly elaborate housing would have to be constructed, not least for food protection.

There is much then for which we must wait to see.

Regional agencies

It remains to mention three operative regional agencies: Intersputnik, ESA, and Arabsat, as other international agencies will be described later.

Intersputnik was established in 1971, designed as an international satellite system. Objections advanced by the USSR to Intelsat, among its reasons for not joining it, were, as might be expected, the ideological opposite of the US objections to the international arrangements just described. In particular, the USSR could not accept management of the system by a private US corporation, or the commercial motivation, represented in particular by the weighting of

[8] The cultivation of plants using, in place of soil, solutions of the mineral salts which the soil normally provides.

votes of member countries on the basis of their share in tele-communication services. The Intersputnik Agreement was concluded in Moscow in November 1971, based on an earlier draft, which was published in 1968 but had not obtained support from COPUOS. The system was to regulate point-to-point telecommunications and also TV broadcasting. The organization was accorded separate legal personality, with the capacity to own and lease space segments, and with the profits realized being distributed among the participating countries in proportion to 'their financial contributions. Membership was declared open to any State. However, it remained limited to the initial signatories,[9] and in fact Cuba, Romania, and the USSR later joined Intelsat.

The European Space Agency Convention, adopted in May 1975, came into force on 30 October 1980, designed to replace ERSO (European Space Research Organization, 1962) and ELDO (European Launcher Development Organization, 1964). Its objects were (Article II):

to provide for and promote, for exclusively peaceful purposes, co-operation among European States in space research and technology and their space applications

and preference was to be given to the use of ESA launchers and other space transport systems, unless they present 'unreasonable disadvantage as compared with other available facilities in terms of cost, reliability and mission suitability' (Article VIII-1). The Agency has separate legal personality, with the capacity, on the unanimous decision of the Council composed of member countries' representatives, to 'co-operate with other international organisations and institutions, and with Governments, organisations and institutions of non-Member States, and conclude agreements with them to this effect' (Article XIV-1). An interesting distinction is made between 'mandatory' and 'optional' activities (Article V-1). Mandatory for member States are, first, programmes approved by a majority of member States, changes requiring a decision by a two-thirds majority, and secondly, the determination of the level of resources, to be made available over

---

[9] Bulgaria, Cuba, Czechoslovakia, German Democratic Republic, Hungary, Mongolia, Poland, Romania, USSR.

five-year periods, requiring unanimity (Article XI-5a). Optional activities may be undertaken on a majority decision. The Agency is to be dissolved if its membership falls below five. ESA has an administrative management and staff.

Eutelsat was established by an interim agreement, which came into force in June 1977, and had been sponsored by the ESA Council. It was concluded between members of CEPT (Comité européen des administations des postes et des télécommunications), and included Finland and Yugoslavia in addition to a majority of Council of Europe countries. Supplementary agreements provided for the financing of the ECS (European Communications Satellite) system, and for the operation of the satellites Marots and Marecs A and B, the latter to be supplied by ESA to Inmarsat (International Maritime Satellite Organization). An Assembly was composed of Eutelsat countries, representatives being member administrations of CEPT or recognized operating agencies. The Agreement also called for a 'reasonable portion of intra-European traffic' through the planned ECS Space Segment. The satellite OTS was launched in May 1978 in geostationary orbit, under the joint responsibility of ESA and Eutelsat, operating at an exceptionally high frequency and providing 7,200 simultaneous telephone calls. Eutelsat became a permanent organization in September 1982.

Arabsat (Arab Satellite Communication Organization) was established by the members of the Arab League in 1976, its purpose being 'to use an Arab satellite as a means of serving the purposes of communications, information, culture, education'. It is structurally similar to the other regional agencies, having the States' Ministers of Communications as the supreme body, a board of nine directors, and a general manager. Financial contributions to operate the system are made by member States, which obtain a proportionate share of the profits. Arabsat concluded a contract with the French Company Aérospatiale for the construction by 1983 of two geostationary satellites and one reserve; these are to operate for seven years, providing 1,700 telephone channels, seven main TV channels, and a community TV channel.

These regional agencies have some notable common features. They avoid the legal tightness of some organizations and, though similar in internal structure to UN specialized agencies, they preserve a pragmatic flexibility, and are in practice partnerships or clubs. Also they are not wholly intergovernmental in function, for their operations must depend on co-operation with national agencies and enterprises, often foreign, through service and supply contracts.

Having reviewed some of the general features of contemporary space activities, we come now to the second part, a consideration of them in greater detail. The principal areas chosen for survey are telecommunications; remote sensing, the rather bizarre expression for Earth surveys; energy sources in outer space; the use of space stations; and the military uses of outer space. The first four areas may be described as administrative, in that they cover space activities, which are devoted primarily to public services, based on governmental and technical administration. They are essentially civil, as distinct from military, uses of outer space, and, though technical in form, are not devoted directly to scientific research. These distinctions do not of course imply that there are fixed frontiers between these various uses of outer space. Spacecraft and space stations may be designed to serve several purposes, and the ambivalence between the civil and military uses of outer space is well known.

Part II

4

Telecommunications

Telecommunications have a long history. Signals and signalling are as old as warfare, and signals for the navy were set out in the Black Book of the Admiralty in 1338. Technical economy and concision have steadily grown along with the increase in range. Nelson's famous signal at the Battle of Trafalgar required the hoisting of thirty-two flags; and in the first electric telegraph system, constructed in 1837, pairs of electrically reflected needles could indicate letters. In the same year Morse devised an electromagnetic telegraph, using his code; and in 1865 an international conference assembled in Paris to consider the use of this system across national boundaries.

Radio-communication, by electromagnetic waves travelling through space—wireless telegraphy—was gradually developed through the nineteenth century in the work of Marconi, Poynting, and Hertz, leading to the establishment by Marconi of a radio-communication system between England and France in 1899. The expansion of radio-communication since then, in range, efficiency, and fields including spacecraft, needs no description here, save to note that its efficiency varies with the power of the transmitter in terms of frequency related to wavelength, and the level of efficiency required also varies necessarily with the purpose for which transmissions are being made. Spacecraft, and particularly Earth satellites, cannot escape these conditions, as they serve as media of telecommunication, and as transmitters of information, and also depend for guidance on radio-communication. Long-wave radio-communication requires larger transmitters and more power than does short wave, but yields signals of higher quality, though short-wave transmission may be more accurately directed. The uses of radio-communication through satellites are wide-ranging, and yet raise a number of problems, some not easy to resolve given their novelty. Among the major issues are the distribution and employment of radio frequencies in satellite communications; the regulation of telecommunications, including forms of broadcasting and, in particular, direct satellite broadcasting; and the distribution of information through satellites, for such purposes as air and sea navigation, weather reporting, and business movements.

Distribution and use of radio-frequencies

The distribution and use of radio-frequencies for satellite telecommunications are governed by the fact that the radio spectrum is a special kind of natural resource. Like many natural resources, it is available to all; but unlike some it may, as an association of electric and magnetic fields, be used indefinitely and is not consumed. It does not then demand the same conservation as non-renewable resources. Nevertheless, radio-frequencies need protection for several reasons: radiation can be subject to kinds of pollution in the form of disturbance by natural or artificial forces, leading to diffraction, absorption, or scattering; frequencies can also be seen to be wastefully used, where there is a special demand for them; and there may be harmful interference with one radio transmission by another. But it is generally accepted that there can be no claim of acquisition of radio waves, as located in space, or of exclusive title to the use of particular frequencies. The radio spectrum is then a *res communes*, already described, and the International Frequencies Registration Board (IFRB) were described in the ITU (Montreux) Convention (1965) as 'custodians of an international public trust' (Article 13).[1]

ITU had established as working principles that there shall be equal access to the radio spectrum for authorized users, and that the use of frequencies shall be notified to ITU, there

---

[1] A Vienna Conference in 1863 established, as a permanent body, the International Bureau of Telegraph Administrations, located in Berne. In 1875 an international Convention revised the 1865 (Paris) Convention and arranged for periodic conferences: these and the Berne Bureau came to be known as the International Telegraph Union, and the International Telecommunications Union from 1948. For an excellent study see David M. Leive, *International Telecommunications and International Law* (Sijthoff, 1970).

being no right, however, to the use of a particular frequency
created simply by the fact of prior notification. It was recognized at the ITU Space Radio-communication Conference in
1963 that the current Radio Regulations (1959) needed
revision of the allocation of frequency bands for the 'various
categories of space communication and radio-astronomy'.

Box 3

The *allocation of frequency bands* is undertaken in ITU radio
conferences, in which the ITU member countries, now over 150,
are represented, bands being allocated to particular telecommunications services: fixed or mobile stations; broadcasting, and air
and sea navigation, services, and so on.

The *assignment of frequencies* to particular stations is the
responsibility of national agencies, but must be notified to the
IFRB.

The *bands of frequencies* range from Very Low Frequency
(VLF) to Very High Frequency (VHF). The VLF band goes from
about 3 to 30 kHz (1 Kilohertz = 1,000 cycles per second), while
the VHF band extends from 30 to 300 GHz (1 gigahertz = 1,000
megahertz = 1,000,000 kilohertz).

The Conference recommended that:

the utilization and exploitation of the frequency spectrum for space
communications be subject to international agreement, based on
principles of justice and equity, permitting the use and sharing of
allocated frequency bands in the mutual interest of all nations.

Revised regulations were attached to the ITU Convention
(1965).

At a World Administrative Radio Conference in 1971,
devoted to space telecommunications, allocations of frequency bands were fixed for communications-satellite
services, and introduced for broadcasting and exploration
services using satellites; and, departing somewhat from the
traditional 'first-come first-served' practice of the IFRB
(International Frequencies Registration Board) in frequency
allocation, the Conference restored that registration of
frequencies used by satellites 'should not provide any permanent priority for any individual country or groups of

countries', and that countries or groups of countries 'should take all practical measures to realize the possibility of the use of new systems' by their countries. In short, the multiplication of competitive systems will set new problems for the ITU and generally for the management of telecommunications satellites; geostationary orbits are already beginning to be crowded by satellites, creating in particular the difficulties of transmission 'spillover', whether intended or not, and the reduction of the number of frequency bands available for allocation.

Regulation of telecommunications

The regulation of telecommunications, apart from the distribution and use of radio-frequencies, has also both national and international forms, and both are prominent in satellite telecommunications.

Domestic telecommunications, so far as they are confined to national territory, are a *domaine réservé* of the State, though some 'spillover' is unavoidable; and they comprise telephone, telex, and radio broadcasting services. But transfrontier transmissions necessarily call for international management, which may be regional in scope or more extended, and may be directed to technical problems such as 'spillover' or to the purpose and content of transmissions. To illustrate, we may see what has been done to establish international systems of management—whilst maintaining some respect for the *domaine réservé* of States—control of 'spillover', and the regulation of broadcasting. We will direct our enquiries to the uses of Earth satellites. We may then offer a general assessment of the management of space telecommunications. We shall describe in turn the establishment and structure of Intelsat, a general system of management, not regionally limited in its functional area; and Inmarsat, a specialized system for aiding marine navigation, and again not regionally limited.

The forces at work in the establishment of Intelsat (International Telecommunications Satellite System) in 1964 were the widening common interest in the development of space telecommunications; the dominance of the US in spacecraft hardware production, launching systems, and operational experience, compelling at least the West European countries to co-operate with it; and at the same time a conflicting desire in some countries, not least France, to compete industrially and in technology.

The main objectives were the co-operative management of telecommunications by satellite in the forms of telephone and telegram services; information services on weather and market prices, and, later, data bank material. A major choice had to be made between a global system and some form of regional organization—ESRO and ELDO were already in existence. In the negotiations the US pressed for a global system, to be managed however by its national corporation, Comsat (Communication Satellite Corporation). A global system was already practicable, given the launch of geosynchronous satellites in 1963, three of which would have the capacity together to provide telecommunication services for most inhabited areas of the world. Management of the proposed system by Comsat, even under some measure of governmental regulation, had understandably strong support in the US Congress and in industry, the latter in any case preferring the leasing of satellite channels to any internationalization of the system. Favoured by some countries however was the establishment of an international organization for satellite telecommunication services, modelled on the specialized agencies of the UN. Its institutional structure would be an assembly, and an executive board, composed of government representatives, the first determining issues of policy and planning in annual meeting, and the second authorized to supervise the practical running of the services, a largely technically qualified secretariat being responsible, under a director-general, for day-to-day management.

Such a system came to be seen as over-ambitious, not least in its placing of satellite telecommunication services under international administration and management. Nineteen countries, at a conference in August 1964, arrived at an interesting compromise.

Two agreements were concluded: Interim Arrangements for a Global Communications Satellite System, registered as an international agreement under Article 102 of the UN Charter; and a Special Arrangement, embodying a contractual arrangement between participating governments and certain public corporations. A provisional International Communications Satellite Committee (ICSC) was also established. The Interim Arrangements had spelt out the objectives as a 'single global commercial communications satellite system' for 'the design, development, construction (including the provision of equipment), establishment, maintenance, operation, and ownership' of the space segment; this was defined as 'the communications satellites, and the tracking, control and related facilities and equipment, required to support the operation of the communication satellites' (Article I (bi)). The space segment was to be owned in undivided shares by the signatories of the Special Arrangement, in proportion to their respective contributions (Article III). The participants, as signatories of the Special Arrangement, could then be governments or a 'communications entity, public or private' designated by a government. Among the latter were Comsat, the Canadian Overseas Telecommunications Corporation, and Kokusai Senshin Denwa Co. in Japan. This mixed participation of public and private enterprise makes for flexibility in operations and management; and a similar policy is reflected in the provisional structure of the Interim Arrangements, which are reminiscent of the General Agreement on Tariff and Trade (GATT), concluded in 1947, in two respects.

First, what is established in effect in both is a consortium or partnership with little formal organization. So in the GATT no distinct institutional body was established, but:

Representatives of the contracting parties shall meet from time to time for the purpose of giving effect to those provisions of this Agreement which involve joint action and, generally, with a view to facilitating and furthering the objectives of this Agreement. Wherever reference is made to this Agreement to the contracting parties acting jointly, they are designated as the CONTRACTING PARTIES (Article XXV).

Further, when Part IV was added to the GATT in 1963, setting out principles, and objectives to be sought, for the benefit of the less-developed contracting parties, it provided that the Contracting Parties were to 'collaborate jointly' to these ends, establishing such 'institutional arrangements as may be necessary' (Article XXVIII-1 and 2(f)). The Interim

Arrangements were similar in not setting up any corporate structures, but assigning the operational tasks of implementing the Agreement to an Interim Communications Satellite Committee—the first Intelsat—to be composed of representatives of signatories of the Special Arrangement.

Secondly, the GATT rested on provisional application in a Protocol, which provides that signatory governments should give notice of provisional application of named parts of the Agreement, and should have also a right to withdraw on sixty days' notice.

The Interim Arrangements for the communications satellite system, though also provisional, were planned out to a greater extent, envisaging (Article I-a):

(i) an experimental and provisional phase, in which it is proposed to use one or more satellites to be placed in geosynchronous orbit in 1965.

(ii) succeeding phases employing satellites, of types to be determined, with the object of achieving basic global coverage in the latter part of 1967.

But, unlike the GATT, which did not expressly provide for any future institutionalization, the Interim Arrangements called for a report, not later than January 1969, from the ICSC, with recommendations concerning 'definitive arrangements', including the possibilities that the interim arrangements be continued on a 'permanent basis' or that a 'permanent international organisation with a General Conference and an international administrative and technical staff' be established (Article IX-a). In fact, despite the growing regional competition in space activities, the first Intelsat grew steadily and over eighty countries were participating when, after two years of negotiation, the Definitive Agreements were concluded in August 1971,[2] entering into force in February 1973, consisting of the Intelsat Agreement with four Annexes and an Operating Agreement with one Annex. The former is an interstate agreement, while the latter is similar to the Special Arrangement in that the parties may be governments or designated communication entities, public or private.

The comparison, novel perhaps, between GATT and

[2] X *International Legal Materials* (1971), 909.

Intelsat is enlightening. The spirit of club and consensus governed GATT, at least in its first decades, because in its area of operation there were conflicts of interest, which it was in the common interest to resolve. These conflicts arose between national trade policies and objectives, shaped by large and not wholly controllable forces. Strict organization of GATT was not practicable,[3] but for Intelsat there was not only a wide common interest in the use and disposition of the results of space and the radio spectrum, without major conflicts, but a need for technical management and administrative decision internationally.

Under the definitive arrangements, Intelsat became an international organization of the kind proposed but rejected in 1964. There is a periodic Assembly of Parties, a Governing Board, and an administration under the Director-General. Though in structure now similar to a UN specialized agency, Intelsat remains a mixed enterprise in that it is a public utility service run on commercial lines, and also combines the functions of governmental agencies and public and private aerospace corporations. The Assembly has a limited recommendatory function, restricted principally to the commercial aspects of Intelsat (Article VII). The Board of Governors, replacing the Interim Communications Satellite Committee, is responsible like its predecessor for the 'design, development, construction, establishment, operation and maintenance' of the Intelsat space segment. There are three categories of governors, who numbered twenty-seven in 1980, and they carry weighted votes in proportion to the investment share of the parties they represent (Article IX).[4] All management and operational functions, the real purpose of Intelsat, are performed by an internationally recruited staff, serving under the Director-General, and replacing Comsat after six years from 1964 (Articles XI and XII).

[3] But the permanent representation of government at its centre in Geneva, its regular trade negotiations, and methods of settlement of trade disputes, have given it a certain structure.

[4] Peak weighting vote is 40 per cent, and decisions may generally be taken by four or more members holding two-thirds of the investment shares. The United States lost its power of veto. Investment shares include, in percentages: US 38.3, UK 10.9, Australia 4.3, Japan 4.1, Canada 3.1, France 3.0, Italy 2.5, FRG 2.4, Pakistan 2.4, Spain 1.8.

Given the increasing size of Intelsat—over one hundred participating telecommunication systems in 1980—its relationship with regional satellite systems had to be determined. Two principles were laid down: that, before the establishment of such a system, the Intelsat Assembly must be consulted, through the Board of Governors, and make recommendations, and that these should be designed

to ensure technical compatibility of such (regional) facilities and their operation with the use of the radio frequency spectrum and orbital space by the existing or planned INTELSAT space segment and to avoid significant economic harm to the global system of INTELSAT (Article XIV).

The Board of Governors adopted certain criteria of economic harm in June 1977 as:

the impact on projected INTELSAT space segment costs and utilization charges, INTELSAT planning and operations, and the resulting impact on signatories' investment

and

the extent to which signatories, not participating in the separate satellite system will have their investment shares increased as a consequence of international public telecommunications traffic or services, which might otherwise have been provided by INTELSAT, being provided by a separate satellite system.

Competition between satellite systems depends in part on comparative costs. Intelsat, like any system, has to cover costs of operations, including use of Earth stations and ground lines, maintenance and administration, and to raise revenue from users of the system; but as an international organization it must distribute charges equitably among its signatories. Intelsat has used 'average cost' pricing, that is, a division of the total costs of the system services among the users in proportion to their use.[5] As the system has advanced technically, it has achieved a reduction in costs. Intelsat V uses digital techniques in 12,000 circuits, operating one-hundred times faster than land-lines; and the rent of a one-way circuit has declined from £13,000 in 1965 to £2,500 in 1980. However, as regards the competition with land-lines,

[5] See P. Passell and L. Ross, *Communications Satellite Tariffs for Television* (International Broadcasting Institute, 1971).

themselves improved by the introduction of fibre optics, the size of Western Europe reduces the advantages of satellite communications, though these continue to be needed for many long-distance communications.

The Convention establishing Inmarsat (International Maritime Satellite Organization) was sponsored by IMCO (Inter-governmental Maritime Consultative Organization), now the International Maritime Organization, and entered into force in July 1979. The purpose of Inmarsat is described in the Convention, and is:

to make provision for the space segment necessary for improving maritime communications, distress and safety of life at sea communications, efficiency and management of ships, maritime public correspondence services and radio determination capabilities (Article 3 (1))

and it must 'act exclusively for peaceful purposes' (Article 3 (3)). The space segment of Inmarsat is defined in terms similar to that of Intelsat, being 'the satellites, and the tracking, telemetry, command, control, monitoring and related facilities and equipment required to support the operation' of the satellites (Article 1(d)). Thirty-seven countries had become parties when operations began in May 1982, with five coastal receiving stations—two each in the US and Japan and one in Norway. Six geosynchronous satellites relay messages between ground stations and ships at sea.

As in Intelsat, it is recognized that the participants in Inmarsat will be telecommunications operators, which may be governmental departments or agencies, or commercial corporations. Each party to the Convention must then designate its operator as the 'competent entity, public or private', subject to its jurisdiction; these 'designated entities' sign the Operating Agreement, which thus has a different legal status from the Convention. For not only are the relations between a party to the Convention and its designated entity governed by its domestic law, but the party is expressly declared not to be 'liable for obligations arising under the Operating Agreement' (Convention, Article 4 (a)). However, the party to the Convention remains responsible for securing observance by the designated entity of obligations arising under the Convention or 'related international agreements' (Article 4 (c)).

The institutional structure of Inmarsat—an Assembly, Council, and Director-General—is similar to that of Intelsat, in the composition and functions of these organs. In the procurement policy to be followed by the Council for the acquisition of goods or services, the requirement of efficiency is to prevail over the principle of an equitable distribution of contracts. The award of contracts for goods and services is to be based on international tenders and made 'to bidders offering the best combination of quality, price and the most favourable delivery time' (Convention, Article 20 (1)). The award of contracts will then go, at least for a time, to the technically more advanced countries. The Intelsat Interim Agreement had endeavoured to resolve the conflict by providing that:

In considering contracts and in exercising their other responsibilities, the Committee and Corporation as manager shall be guided by the need to design, develop and procure the best equipment and services at the best price for the most efficient conduct and operation of the space segment.

But given any comparability of tenders in these terms, they:

shall also seek to ensure that contracts are so distributed . . . in approximate proportion to the respective quotas of their corresponding signatories to the Special Agreement (Article X).

It is difficult to see how, in either system, the distribution of contracts in proportion to quotas could alter the market predominance of the United States.[6]

A major problem in the management of telecommunications is 'spillover', or radiation or emission, particularly in the form of broadcasting, over the territory of other countries. It can constitute harmful interference, in that, in the language of the ITU Regulations, it obstructs or constantly interrupts or degrades a radio-communication service that is being operated in conformity with the ITU Radio Regulations. Spillover may be reduced or prevented by technical measures in the country of transmission, or by the ITU setting distance

---

[6] Principal initial quotas of investment in Inmarsat were, in percentages: US 23.5, USSR 14.1, UK 9.9, Norway 7.9, Japan 7.0.

limits, co-ordinating the various transmissions, or by an agree-ment of tolerance between the countries concerned. In space activities spillover can have a number of challengeable forms:[7] harmful interference with transmissions from other spacecraft or Earth stations, or with communications between spacecraft and Earth stations. Distance limits are not easy to set for such transmissions, and has adapted its Radio Regulations to satellite broadcasting thus:

In devising the characteristics of a space station in the Broadcasting-Satellite Service, all technical means available shall be used to reduce, to the maximum extent practicable, the radiation over the territory of other countries unless an agreement has been previously reached with such countries.

Where the spillover is deliberate, we have direct satellite broadcasting, to be described later.

Apart from the ITU Regulations, regional control of spillover is possible. So there was provision in the North American Broadcasting Agreement (1960) that the signals from any foreign station at the border of the United States should not exceed a prescribed maximum strength, and that no foreign station within 650 miles of the border should operate at night.

In effect, within the virtually global ITU system, any transmitted broadcast is proscribed if this transmission is technically avoidable and has not received the consent of the State into which it comes. It may be seen then as a form of trespass or nuisance, or, given the content of the broad-cast, as an interference in internal affairs. This leads to the con-flict over direct satellite broadcasting, to be discussed below.

Management of radio and TV broadcasting

This raises many problems, national and international, and massive in the use of satellites: for example, how far should it be a public monopoly; whether land-lines or satellites are to be preferred as channels; how radio pirates are to be controlled; and possible rules for transfrontier broadcasting.[8]

---

[7] See generally Leive, op. cit.

[8] For a general survey see M. Faristen, 'Le Début sur les Radios Locales', *La Documentation Française* 354 (19.1.1979).

In France, legislation from 1959 to 1974 established radio broadcasting as a public monopoly. So:

La radiodiffusion-télévision française est placée sous l'autorité du Ministre chargé de l'information. Elle constitue un éstablissment public d'Etat, à caractère industriel et commercial, doté d'un budget autonome.

In the United Kingdom, the original monopoly of the BBC under its Charter was first reduced by the creation of the Independent Television Authority in 1954, and then terminated in 1972 by the establishment by statute of the Independent Broadcasting Authority (IBA), absorbing the ITA. However, while the production of programmes by individuals or groups for independent broadcasting is not under direct public control, the competent Minister has power to require the broadcasting of governmental communications, and to forbid the broadcasting through the IBA of a particular programme, or a category of programmes, and its broadcasting is also subject to time restrictions. In federal systems the divisions of authority and responsibility will be greater.

The ESA is at present planning a series of five satellites, called L-SAT, and modelled on ECS, to begin operations in 1988. Meanwhile there is a consortium from the FRG and France planning two independent satellites to operate from 1984.[9] But we know that development plans are often abandoned. Competition takes many larger forms as between, for example, Intelsat and regional satellite systems. This was recognized in the conclusion of the Definitive Agreements and a certain compromise was reached, based on two principles. First, countries participating in Intelsat undertake, before establishing a regional system, to consult the Assembly of Parties through the Board of Governors; and the Assembly is to express 'in the form of recommendation its findings regarding the considerations set out'. Further, these recommendations are:

to ensure technical compatibility of such (regional) facilities and their operation with the use of the radio frequency spectrum and orbital space by the existing or planned INTELSAT space segment, and to avoid significant economic harm to the global system of INTELSAT.

[9] Aerospatiale-Thomson: Messerschmitt-Bolker-Blohm; AEG Telefunken.

In practice, reconciliation of interests and some collaboration between Intelsat and regional systems has been achieved: for example, in 1980 Intelsat decided to order two Ariane launchings by the ESA of satellites in the Intelsat series. However, Intelsat has assumed little responsibility for European services, and the recommendation by its Governing Board that ECS 1 and 2, operated by Eutelsat, be discontinued from 1988, shows a spirit of economic competition. The natural range of radio-transmissions makes broadcasting from outside national territories a possible practice demanding some control, whether it is public or private.

Whether 'pirate' broadcasting through satellites will be undertaken and become a nuisance remains to be seen. 'Pirate' broadcasting is characterized essentially by the location of its source, it consists of transmissions from stations outside national territories, and consequently it is to be assumed not to be authorized by any State jurisdiction. In 1959 the WARC (World Administratative Radio Conference) of ITU adopted Regulation 422 which provided that:

The establishment and use of broadcasting stations (sound broadcasting and television broadcasting stations) on board ships aircraft, or any other floating or airborne objects outside national territories, is prohibited.

The ITU also sponsored a convention in 1965 committing parties not to provide any assistance to pirate broadcasting stations. In the same year an agreement was adopted in the Council of Europe,[10] which entered into force in 1967 and used the definition of pirate broadcasting in Radio Regulation 422. But its provisions strengthened the means of prohibition by requiring that the establishment or operation of such broadcasting stations, and acts of collaboration with them, be all made punishable offences. It is generally supposed, that, given their terms and scope, these international agreements cannot be extended directly to broadcasting through satellites. But the European Agreement could without great changes be used as a model for a global convention to deal with pirate broadcasting through satellites. Further, it is

[10] European Agreement for the Prevention of Broadcasts transmitted from Stations outside National Territories.

possible that this Agreement might be combined with the earlier European Agreement on the Protection of Television Broadcasts (1961) to prevent the rediffusion of satellite broadcasts from ground stations outside national territory.

It is direct satellite broadcasting which has raised perhaps the greatest controversy over the uses of outer space. Let us describe it.

Direct satellite broadcasting

In satellite broadcasting, programme signals go from the transmitter to the satellite (up-link), which is equipped to amplify and retransmit them back to Earth (down-link). Normally this is to a ground station, which is either incorporated in a radio retransmitter or linked to it by coaxial cable, so that the programme signals are retransmitted as radio or TV broadcasts. The WARC in 1971 considered the possible forms of 'direct reception by the general public' of satellite broadcasting, and distinguished, on the one hand, 'community reception' by fairly complex receivers for 'a group of the general public at one location' or 'through a distribution system covering a limited area'; and on the other hand, 'individual reception' by 'simple domestic installations' or home reception.

As regards direct and semi-direct transmission, there are important differences between community reception and home reception in scale, programmes, and costs. Community reception is limited in location, there being generally a single group of listeners or viewers in a school or village, or redistribution by cable to receivers for such groups over a relatively small region. Reception and redistribution can also be restricted or controlled. Again community reception will be largely for special programmes, providing forms of education or training, information on, for example, agricultural methods, and guidance in health services. Community reception of this kind is already in extensive use, such programmes being of special interest and concern in developing countries. India embarked on a TV satellite project, with the assistance of the United States, and the use of community receivers

Box 4

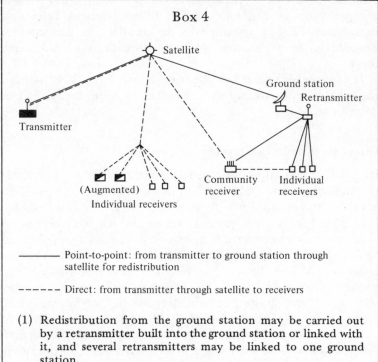

Point-to-point: from transmitter to ground station through satellite for redistribution

Direct: from transmitter through satellite to receivers

(1) Redistribution from the ground station may be carried out by a retransmitter built into the ground station or linked with it, and several retransmitters may be linked to one ground station.

(2) Direct transmission may be achieved by augmenting individual receivers with a dish-type aerial, at some cost; or through an increase in power with immediate reception in 'home sets'.

(3) Direct transmission to community receivers, for redistribution to individual receivers, for example in schools or homes, may be described as semi-direct, and has advantages for many countries.

was designed to reduce language differences.[11] Home receivers are not only located throughout whole countries but the programmes directed to them are not generally particularly specialized. A further critical factor is that the reception of satellite broadcasting programmes in home receivers cannot be prevented or restricted as it can in community receivers,

[11] About 35 per cent of the population of India speak Hindi, while four other languages are each spoken by not less than 10 per cent of the population.

or retransmission channels. However, home reception calls for, and will for some time depend on, the amplification of receivers by the installation of larger antennae, frequency conversion, or other means, and this is expensive. Thus for various reasons, community reception is likely to predominate in the developing countries.

But the possibility of direct satellite broadcasting into home receivers, nearer perhaps in technology and time in the industrialized countries, has created anxieties. In terms of the international conventions and declarations, it presents a conflict between the freedom to impart and receive information and the principle of non-intervention in the environment or internal affairs of other countries. The UN and its agencies have for many years addressed themselves to the problem, and it will be convenient to consider direct satellite broadcasting first in the general context of the international regulation of broadcasting.

The tendency in regulation has been to concentrate on the control of distribution rather than on interference with programme content. The Convention on Distribution of Programme-carrying Signals by Satellite (1979) has been referred to above with its definition of 'programmes' and 'signals'.[12] In was ratified, when it came into force, by the Federal Republic of Germany, Kenya, Mexico, Nicaragua, and Yugoslavia—an interesting range of countries. Programme content comes into account only in the exception made for developing countries, which are not required to prohibit distribution of a programme under the Convention, where it is 'solely for the purpose of teaching, including teaching in the framework of adult education, or scientific research' (Article 4 (iii)). The purpose of the Convention was essentially to prevent 'poaching' of satellite programmes, for unauthorized redistribution could impinge the rights of broadcasters and performers, particularly in respect of copyright: hence the sponsorship of WIPO. But the Convention provisions imply generally that the transmission of satellite broadcast programmes across national boundaries needs intergovernmental agreement. The European Agreement on the Protection of Television Broadcasts is

[12] See pp. 30-1.

similar.[13] Under its provisions TV broadcasting organizations have, in respect of all their TV broadcasts (Article 1 (1)):

the right to authorise or prohibit . . .
  (b) the diffusion of such broadcasts to the public by wire;
  (c) the communication of such broadcasts to the public by means of any instrument for the transmission of signs, sounds or images;
  (d) any fixation of such broadcasts or still photographs thereof, and any reproduction of such a fixation.

This assertion of the domestic jurisdiction over broadcasting is reflected in the notion of prior consent to transmission across national boundaries. The WARC adopted Regulation 428A in 1971, that:

In devising the characteristics of a space-station in the broadcasting-satellite service, all technical means available shall be used to reduce, to the maximum extent practicable, the radiation over the territory of other countries unless an agreement has been reached with such countries.

The scope of this Regulation is not wholly clear: it may be asked, first, whether it relates to equal broadcasting operations or is limited to the design and production of the broadcasting-satellite equipment; and, secondly, whether in any case the reduction of radiation is confined to 'spillover'. That the latter was the intention is indicated by the reference in the WARC in 1977 to its Plan for broadcasting-satellite services:

The Conference decided in principle that the planning of the Broadcasting-Satellite Service in this band should be for domestic broadcasting. In only a few cases, and then only when agreement was specifically given at the Conference, does the Plan enable direct inter-country broadcasting on the same channels. Spillover has been reduced to a minimum consistent with No. 428A of the Radio Regulations.

A degree of 'spillover' from satellite broadcasting, greater than from ordinary broadcasting, is perhaps unavoidable given its geographical scale. TV broadcasting by satellite also presents technical problems. In 1977 the WARC allocated five channels for use by direct broadcasting satellites, in the frequency band around 12 GHz. Frequency counters have been designed to bring the frequency of programme signals

---

[13] It entered into force in 1961, protocols being added in 1965 and 1974. Ten countries had become parties to it by 1980 including the United Kingdom.

down to 1 GHz or below, yielding better quality presentation but less accurately directed signals. There are also difficulties of choice between standards of image-definition and of colour.

The notion of prior consent to broadcasting across national boundaries has prevailed in governmental thinking, and with the advent of direct satellite broadcasting there have also been moves towards control of the contents of broadcast programmes.[14] Draft conventions have been put forward by a number of countries including the USSR, France, Canada, Sweden, and Argentina, but no convention has yet been adopted governing direct satellite broadcasting. Prior consent to broadcasting from foreign sources is called for in these draft conventions for TV broadcasting: USSR Article VI-1, and Canada–Sweden Principles V and VI. The latter read:[15]

Direct television broadcasting by satellite to any foreign State shall be undertaken only with the consent of that State. The consenting State shall have the right to participate in activities which involve coverage of territory under its jurisdiction and control. This participation shall be governed by appropriate international arrangements between the States involved.

The right of consent and participation stated in Principle V shall apply in those cases:
(a) where coverage of the territory of a foreign State entails radiation of a satellite signal beyond the limits considered technically unavoidable under the Radio Regulations of the ITU;
(b) where notwithstanding the technical unavoidability of spillover to the territory of a foreign State, the satellite broadcast is aimed specifically at an audience in that State within the area of the spillover.

The set of principles proposed by Argentina was not limited to television, but stated that: 'In cases where direct broadcasts by satellite are intended for a foreign State, express prior consent is required; the possibility of tacit or extemporaneous consent is not acceptable in such cases.' The formulations are, in part, questionable, for to make consent

[14] An ample study of the development of direct satellite broadcasting and of attitudes to it, including the texts of the draft conventions, is Kathryn M. Queeney, *Direct Broadcasting Satellites and the UN* (Sijthoff, 1978).
[15] Quoted from Queeney, op. cit.

to reception of broadcasting an absolute condition is, given the scope of satellite broadcasting, plainly impracticable; and the application of the rule of avoidability recognizes this. However, two useful principles are enunciated: first, that States, into which a satellite broadcast may come, shall participate in the 'activities', that is presumably the planning and construction of the broadcast; and, secondly, that it is the aim and intent of the broadcast, revealed in its content, that can make it unacceptable to the receiving State. But the fact that these principles have not yet reached embodiment in a general international convention points to the controversy they arouse.

International attempts to introduce some control over the contents of broadcast programmes began with the Convention on the Use of Broadcasting in the Cause of Peace (1936), which prohibited broadcasting that incited war, revolution, or armed revolt, or endangered internal state security or order. The second condition, a major element in the controversy over direct satellite broadcasting, might be seen as imposing too great a limitation on broadcasting; and the General Assembly Resolution 110–II (3 November 1947) followed the Convention (1936) in condemning all propaganda designed or likely to provoke or encourage any threat to the peace, breach of the peace, or act of aggression, but it was not extended to cover the internal affairs of States. This Resolution is declared in the preamble to the Outer Space Treaty (1967) to be applicable to outer space and activities there; and following the General Assembly Resolutions, including one establishing a Working Group on satellite broadcasting, Unesco, in General Conference in November 1972, adopted a Declaration of Guiding Principles on the Use of Satellite Broadcasting. Here the conflict between freedom to impart and receive information and the principle of non-intervention, linked to the notion of prior consent, begins clearly to emerge. The Convention states that 'Satellite broadcasting shall respect the sovereignty and equality of all States' (Article I–1), and to secure the objectives set out in the Declaration, including the 'free flow of information', the 'spread of education', and the 'promotion of cultural exchange', it is necessary that States taking into account the principle of freedom of information, reach or promote prior agreements concerning direct satellite broadcasting to the population of countries other than the country of origin of the transmission (Article IX–1).

but:

Each country has the right to decide on the content of the educational programs broadcast by satellite to its people and, in cases where such programs are produced in cooperation with other countries, to take part in their planning and production, on a free and equal footing (Article VI–2)

and 'in the preparation of programmes for direct broadcasting to other countries, account shall be taken of differences in the national laws of the countries of reception' (Article X).

Can the notion of prior consent to direct satellite broadcasting be linked to the principle of non-intervention? A general statement on that principle was made in the Final Act of the Conference on Security and Cooperation in Europe at Helsinki (1975); from which Principle VI reads:

The participating States will refrain from any intervention, direct or indirect, individual or collective, in the internal or external affairs falling within the domestic jurisdiction of another participating State, regardless of their mutual relations.

They will accordingly refrain from any form of armed intervention or threat of such intervention against another participating State.

They will likewise in all circumstances refrain from any act of military, or of political, economic or other coercion designed to subordinate to their own interest the exercise by another participating State of the rights inherent in its sovereignty and thus to secure advantages of any kind.

Accordingly they will *inter alia* refrain from direct or indirect assistance to terrorist activities, or to subversive or other activities directed towards the violent overthrow of the regime of another participating State.

On the other side of the coin is the International Covenant on Civil and Political Rights, which came into force in 1976. Article 19 provides that:

2. Everyone shall have the right to freedom of expression; this right shall include freedom to seek, receive and impart information and ideas of all kinds, regardless of frontiers, either orally, in writing or in print, and in the form of art, or through any other media of his choice.

The disregard of frontiers here is not perhaps as bold as it sounds, for it is giving expression both to the expansion of technology, and to the decline of sovereign independence —no state can any longer limit communications over its territory. How far, then, given the principle of non-intervention, can direct satellite broadcasting be used to exercise freedom of information?[16]

There is much to explore here. Let us assume for this purpose that a programme is transmitted through satellite from the country of origin by an authorized broadcaster, that the programme is intended for audiences in the receiving country—we are not dealing here with any question of spillover—that the programme is direct in that it may enter community or home receivers from the satellite, that there has been no agreement on such transfrontier broadcasting between the two countries, and that they are both parties to the Civil and Political Rights Covenant. We have first two broad questions to ask: can the receiving country restrict or prevent the reception of the programme and be consistent with Article 19 of the Covenant; and can it invoke the principle of non-intervention against the country of origin?

It is clear that under Article 19 (2), the transmission and reception of a broadcast programme are exercises of the freedom to impart and to receive information and ideas, that a national frontier cannot be in itself an obstacle to the satellite broadcast, which is also a medium that is available and open to the choice of the individual listener or viewer. Direct satellite broadcasting is then covered by these provisions of the Covenant. But freedom of information, like almost all declared human rights, is subject to permissible restrictions. So Article 19 (3) states that:[17]

The exercise of the rights provided for in paragraph 2 of this Article carries with it special duties and responsibilities. It may therefore be subject to certain restrictions, but these shall only be such as are provided by law and are necessary:

[16] See C. G. Fenwick, 'The Use of Radio as an Instrument of Foreign Propaganda', 32 *American Journal of International Law* (1938), 341.
[17] European Convention on Human Rights, Article 10 (2) is similar.

(a) for respect of the rights and reputations of others;
(b) for the protection of national security or of public order (ordre public) or of public health or morals.

The effectiveness of such restrictions on direct satellite broadcasting would appear to be limited. Domestic restrictions could be imposed in the country from which programmes were transmitted by satellite, making disregard of certain standards of programme content a ground for withdrawal of the licence to operate the satellite. But to show that they were justified in respect of transmissions to another country would be difficult.

Consider two situations, the first, in which the broadcast is being received both in the country of transmission and in another country; and the second, in which the programme is designed for, and is in fact received, only in the other country. In the first situation, an objection to the programme from the second country may be met by the claim that its broadcast is in the interest of the people in the country of transmission. But there is again some difference, between a programme of general character with only indirect effects in the second country, and one which touches specifically on internal conflicts within it. Given the latter, the second country could possibly justify restrictions imposed on the domestic reception of the programme under Article 19 (3); but a trimming of the transmission which extended to interference with reception of the broadcast in the country of transmission, would certainly be harmful interference.

The country of reception has then some room for manœuvre to restrict direct satellite broadcasting into its territory for the protection of national security or public order, or public health or morals. There is understandably most concern with the first two grounds of restriction, since they lie most within the discretion of government, and can be the base for the abuse of power.

It is in the second situation, of a programme designed for the second country, that the greater difficulties arise. Can any reliance be placed on the principle of non-intervention, and a related requirement of prior consent to such transfrontier broadcasting?

The prerequisite of prior consent has been debated at length in COPUOS, by its Working Group and Legal Committee, without any resolution of the problem in the form of an international convention. This inconclusive debate points, on the one hand, to a lack of confidence in the Civil and Political Rights Covenant as a basis of either protection or restriction of direct satellite broadcasts, and, on the other, to the difficulty of resolving the conflicts of interest that arise. So, as regards a requirement of prior consent, certain governments, calling in their draft proposals for its inclusion in any declaration or convention concerning direct satellite broadcasting, did not appear to present any rationale for it, though there were vague invocations of sovereignty. But if sovereignty here is to be understood as meaning an exclusive right or jurisdiction over the reception of broadcasts in state territory, it cannot itself be either the basis or explanation of a right to require and give prior consent; for the bare statement that the right of prior consent is a sovereign right is, like many statements involving sovereignty, a circularity: what is in effect being said is that the reception of broadcasts in State territory is within its exclusive jurisdiction because it is within its sovereignty, that is, its exclusive jurisdiction.

The Unesco Declaration of Guiding Principles on the Use of Space Broadcasting for the Free Flow of Information, the Spread of Information and Greater Cultural Exchange[18] calls on States 'to reach or promote prior agreements concerning direct satellite broadcasting to the population of countries other than the country of origin of the transmission' but presented no reasons to explain it.

Can the content of the broadcast programme, as distinct from the technical features of its transmission and reception, or its purpose, be said to constitute another kind of harmful interference, so that the absence of prior consent to it by the receiving State entitles it to take counteraction, including perhaps even the destruction of the satellite? The principle of non-intervention is directed against interference from one State in another, which is in some way acceptable or injurious.

[18] UN Doc. A/AC105/109 (15.11.1972).

The debates in the UN, which culminated in Resolution 2625-XXV (24 October 1970),[19] reflected different approaches to the principle of non-intervention, based on differing political attitudes; and it is these of course that will shape the kinds of broadcast in the second situation. If these political attitudes can be polarized, without too great distortion, as liberal and socialist, the first expressing the ideas of liberal democracy and the second those of planned often authoritarian societies, then the liberal approach will in general favour intervention, falling short of the use of force, at least for the protection of human rights; but in the socialist approach this will be opposed as a denial of political independence, or in the words of Brezhnev, part of 'strategic plans against the world of socialism'. As a compromise between two approaches, we find in a statement of principle in the Helsinki Final Act the critical phrase prohibiting intervention in 'the internal and external affairs falling within the domestic jurisdiction' of another participating State. This is the most recent expression of a historic phrase, but how it is to be understood is not altogether clear.

In Article 2 (7) of the UN Charter, the UN is precluded from intervening save under Chapter VII (Action with respect to Threats to the Peace, Breaches of the Peace, and Acts of Aggression) in 'matters which are essentially within the domestic jurisdiction of any State'. The term 'essentially', which takes the place of 'solely' in the equivalent provision in the League of Nations Covenant, can be taken as meaning that some matters may be within the domestic jurisdiction of a State but of sufficient international concern to justify intervention by the UN by way at least of debate, recommendations, and even admonition. So the duty of the UN under the Charter 'to promote . . . universal respect for, and observance of, human rights and fundamental freedoms for all without distinction as to race, sex, language or religion' (Article 55), and the 'pledge' of UN members to take 'joint and separate action in cooperation' with the UN to achieve these purposes (Article 56), have been taken to imply that

---

[19] This declaration on the rights and duties of States includes: 'No State or group of States has the right to intervene directly or indirectly, for any reason whatever, in the internal or external affairs of any other State.'

intervention is justifiable for the protection of human rights. In effect then, while the respect for, and observance of, human rights are secured in domestic law and practice, they can no longer be regarded as internal affairs essentially within the domestic jurisdiction. But are they in that sense 'external affairs falling within the domestic jurisdiction', and consequently still guarded from intervention under Principle VI of the Helsinki Final Act? Whatever this rather odd notion of 'external affairs falling within the domestic jurisdiction' is designed to cover, it would be difficult to exclude from it human rights, when seen as matters of international concern. Further, Principle VII, repeating in substance Articles 55 and 56 of the UN Charter, sets out in some detail the commitments of the participating states to respect and observe human rights with reference to the International Civil and Political Rights Covenant and the Economic, Social and Cultural Rights Covenant. More particularly, among the fields of co-operation envisaged in the Helsinki Final Act are 'Space exploration and the study of the earth's natural resources and the natural environment by remote sensing in particular with the assistance of satellites and rocket-probes'; and the participating States 'will favour cooperation among public or private, national or international radio and television organisations, through the exchange of both live and recorded radio and television programmes, and through the joint production and the broadcasting and distribution of such programmes'.

The Helsinki Final Act then, though it is a contemporary and influential declaration of principles of government and international relations, gives no clear guidance on direct satellite broadcasting. It is not perhaps surprising that the tactical need to accommodate markedly different attitudes in the declarations was met formally not only by stressing that the Final Act was not an international agreement but also by stating that:

All the principles set forth above are of primary significance and, accordingly, they will be equally and unreservedly applied, each of them being interpreted taking into account the others.

It may be concluded then that, at least for the countries that have ratified the Civil and Political Rights Covenant, the right of individuals to seek, impart, and receive information through direct satellite broadcasting must in principle prevail over any rule of non-intervention or prior consent as between States; and that this right can be restricted only where the content of the programme can be clearly shown to weaken national security in the receiving State, or to injure reputations. But in practice countries will no doubt, in the interest of co-operation, seek prior agreement over broadcasting by satellites.[20]

Information services

The expansion of information technology embraces satellites, which are providing information services of two kinds: the communication and exchange of information, similar to postal and telephone services; and the accumulation and accessibility of data.

Technical developments have in the last decade been rapid. The Prestel enterprise in the United Kingdom has already established an information service—videotext—operated through TV sets in a large number of offices and homes, linked to centralized computers by telephone lines. Data processing, for storage or for communication as information —'data' and 'information' are often used as interchangeable terms—is performed by machinery, including computers, in which the input of data is subjected to arithmetical and logical operations. The capacity of the computer depends upon the units of information it can absorb. A 'bit' is a unit of information, composed either of single figures or numerals, in, for example, binary notation using 1 and 0, or alternatively of physical quantities of electric voltage or resistance; the first are called *digital* and the second *analogue*.

The use of Earth satellites in such information services has begun. Ethernet, a local network of office link-ups by satellite, is operating in the United States supported by a number of firms including British ICI; the US enterprise Satellite Business Systems, owned by IBM, has, in collaboration with British Telecom International, a satellite system

[20] See generally on satellite broadcasting, Delbert D. Smith, *Communication via Satellite* (Sijthoff, 1970).

working with ground stations in Illinois and at Madley, near Hereford, in the United Kingdom; and British Teletext, including business news (Keyfax), is being broadcast by satellite over the United States. Eutelsat, which became a permanent organization in September 1982 and is composed of nineteen European telecommunications administrations, is planning to operate similar systems through ECS (European Communications Satellites) and by purchase of units in the French Telecom 1, to be launched in 1984. The 'teleconference' is now on.

These developments illustrate further the expanding role of private commercial enterprise in satellite operations, and also characteristically broaden the problems posed by data banks. This term is conveniently concise, but it must be remembered that it comprises both the storage of data, sometimes secret, and the collection of information for its communication. The Council of Europe addressed itself to the problems in Resolutions adopted in 1973 and 1974.[21] Though they do not mention the use of Earth satellites as data banks, they set down certain leading principles that are applicable to data banks, whatever their form. So Resolution (74) 29 states that:

2. The information stored should be:
   (a) obtained by lawful and fair means;
   (b) accurate and kept up to date;
   (c) appropriate and relevant to the purpose for which it has been stored.

Lawfulness requires that data banks shall be 'provided for by law, or by special regulation, or have been made public in a statement or document in accordance with the legal system of each member State'. Further:

5. Every individual should have the right to know the information stored about him. Any exception to this principle or limitation to the exercise of this right should be strictly regulated.
6. (b). Electronic data banks should be equipped with security systems which bar access to the data held by them to persons not entitled to obtain such information, and which provide for the detection of misdirections of information, whether intentional or not.

[21] F. W. Hondius, *Emerging Data Protection in Europe*, is a most useful study of both practice and principles.

But Earth satellites, as vehicles of storage and communication of data, override national sovereignties and can escape such legal controls by their scale of operation. Even though legislation is passed in a country, which gives effect to these principles and covers electronic data banks in satellites, and such satellites remain under the jurisdiction and control of that country, as the State of registry, it does not follow that access to its data from another country can be governed by that legislation. Again, while the ITU Convention (1975) gives States the right to stop telegraphic communications for reasons of national security or to ensure compliance with the law, or to maintain 'public order and decency' (Article 32), communications from and with satellites are at present difficult to interrupt; and the structural difficulties have been described in a UN report:[22]

The equipment of electronic data processing is largely in the hands of new, mostly un-regulated enterprises while the equipment for moving the data from computer to user is largely in the hands of the traditional, publicly-owned or regulated common carriers ... This situation is considered by some to complicate regulatory efforts ... particularly where . . . the data-processing equipment is foreign owned or even physically located outside the borders of the country receiving information.

Only international agreements can resolve the problems, but proposals for an international convention to regulate the use of Earth satellites for storage and communication of information have not yet matured.

[22] E/CN4/1142 Addendum 2, p. 16, quoted in Leive, op. cit.

5

Remote Sensing

Remote sensing is a curious phrase, suggesting some delicate process of eye or ear rather than the massive mechanism and unprecedented range of satellite observation. Oceanography and geology, the World Weather Watch, the location of vital resources on land and on sea, the disposition and movement of armed forces, and the anticipation of natural disasters, are all within its reach. Remote sensing potentially stands, not least for the Third World, as one of the greatest human advances in history.

It has been broadly described as 'a system for measuring environmental conditions at or within a few meters of the surface of the Earth by means of airborne and orbital electromagnetic sensors'.[1] Among environmental conditions are crop acreage; timber volume and forest fires; location of surface water; ice cover and movement in Polar regions; geophysical patterns including land movements; mineral resources; the movement of fish stocks; and air and water pollution; and cartography is another product of satellite surveys.[2] The reference to airborne must also be noticed. COPUOS has described remote sensing by balloons and sounding-rockets, which have not the range of satellites but are capable of small-scale observations and have, above all, the advantage of low cost; for example, it is reported that in France four balloon-survey missions producing 1,000 images cost only about $10,000. These balloons, carrying cameras and photometers, could operate at an altitude of 35 km, far higher than aircraft, and cover an area of 625 km^2 to a detail (picture element or 'pixel') of 1:400,000, concentrating on water

[1] UN Doc. A/AC105/118 (12.6.1973). A general review is US National Academy of Sciences, *Resource Sensing from Space: Prospects for Developing Countries* (1977).

[2] Less than half of the developing countries have been mapped above the scale of 1 inch = about 16 miles.

resources and pollution, forestry, and agriculture. Sounding-rockets in the United Kingdom, Skylark and Petrel, though providing only a short time for observations, have taken photographs of areas up to 20,000 km². Satellites, though far more costly, have in contrast a broad overview of large areas, periodic coverage, negligible distortion of the recorded image, and multispectral scanning. The Landsat series of Earth Resources Technology Satellites (ERTS) has already demonstrated this. The first was launched by the United States in 1972, and Landsat D, launched in July 1982, operates in near circular, Polar orbits, at altitudes of around 700 to 900 km. Fourteen terrestrial revolutions are made daily so that the satellite passes over the source area at the same local time every eighteen days. Two observation systems are carried; the scale of observation has been increased by progressive reduction of the size of identifiable areas and objects. Transmissions are passed through NASA; tracking and data relay satellite orbiting at an altitude of 36,000 km. The sale of Landsat to private enterprise is envisaged.

Box 5

The two observation systems are a 'return beam vidicon', and a four-band multispectral scanner, or 'thematic mapper'. The former generates radiation which, after interaction with the object, returns a signal recorded on magnetic tape for computer analysis. The 'thematic mapper' causes solar radiation, reflected back from the object by means of an oscillating mirror, to fall on a bank of sensors and be recorded in four bands of the visible and near infra-red spectrum. The sensors count the images into digital form for transmission to ground stations.

The area of coverage of the first system has been about 185 km², and the smallest identifiable area ('pixel'), originally 79 m², or more than ten times smaller than could be observed from balloons, has now been reduced by Landsat D to 30 m². The 'thematic mapper' of Landsat covers areas down to about 1,000 m², its predecessor having covered 5,000 m².

Receiving stations for Landsat have been established in the United States, Canada, Brazil, and Italy, and are under construction in Iran, Zaïre, Chile, and Argentina; and images are processed and stored at the Earth Resources Observation Systems (EROS) Data Center at Sioux Falls, South Dakota. Images are purchasable on demand, and though charges were doubled in 1982, purchases still came from over 120 countries. This commercial element is perhaps a reason for the transfer, which was proposed for 1983, from NASA to the US Department of Commerce of these environmental satellite services. There have been indications that Landsat has been recently running at a loss.

Other countries are introducing remote-sensing services, in which technical and commercial competition is evident. The ESA plans an Earth Resources Satellite (ERS) series to commence operations in 1987, under the direction of a Remote Sensing Programme Board. In the first phase ERS 1 will survey sea areas, and monitor the movements of fish, oil pollution, the wave levels, and the management of ice. A second phase, not yet fully opened and to be in about 1989, would undertake land surveys, where smaller 'pixel' areas are called for than in sea surveys, so requiring higher frequencies. The detection of crop diseases and the growth of forests would be among the targets, and ERS 1 will, unlike Landsat, be able to 'see' through clouds by obtaining radar images from, for example, wave movements. Two international consortia are competing for the ERS 1 contract, and Eurospace, a group of companies, reported in 1980 that:

Application systems using modern European technologies will soon become operational and generate income for exports. However, at this stage no new major programme is defined, and the budget and terms of reference for ESA are in question.[3]

National enterprise is variable. The United Kingdom has in recent years spent about half on space activities of that spent by either France or the Federal Republic of Germany. The budget of the Centre Nationale d'Études Spatiales (CNES) has been increased for the mid-1980s, and Spot Image, a company owned as to one-third by CNES, plans the production of two remote-sensing satellites, to be launched by CNES in 1984 and 1986. Some of the hardware of both satellites and the ground network are to be supplied from

³ In *New Scientist* (19.6.1980).

Belgium and Sweden, a proportion of shares in Spot Image being reserved for companies in those countries. Images recorded will be purchasable from the control station near Toulouse, and also from ground stations in the United States, Sweden, Australia, Brazil, Upper Volta, and Bangladesh, which will pay annual royalties to CNES. Satellite pictures will be taken of areas of 60 km^2, and the 'pixel' level will be brought down to 10 m.

The principles that have come to be accepted to govern the use of remote-sensing satellites depend necessarily on their functions. A number of rights and obligations recognized in international law come into account, and may in conventional language be described as the extent of exclusive State jurisdiction, and freedom of information. There are of course also the environmental effects of space operations, which are disclosed in remote sensing.

State jurisdiction

Can a country invoke exclusive State jurisdiction in order to prevent or limit remote sensing of its territory by a foreign satellite, and can the information obtained be itself regarded as a natural resource over which it has sovereignty?

There is first the notion of trespass in foreign territory by overflight or by surface surveying, in some sense more so than with the passage of a telecommunications satellite. The ICAO Convention recognizes, subject to certain conditions, a right of overflight by aircraft, which are not engaged in scheduled international air services (Article 5), which is similar to innocent passage of vessels in the territorial sea. But the overflight of pilotless aircraft requires special authorization (Article 8). The Outer Space Treaty is silent on the overflight of spacecraft, though its broad language in Articles 2 and 3 suggests that the principle of innocent passage applies. A satellite in orbit is not of course covered by the ICAO Convention, which is concerned with aircraft operating in airspace, but a space shuttle may be such an aircraft at certain stages of its flight.

While the ICAO Convention allows the prohibition, or regulation by a State of the use of photographic apparatus in aircraft over its territory (Article 36), that surface surveying by satellite is not itself a trespass is implied by Outer Space Treaty, Article 11, where it is sufficient 'to inform the Secretary General of the United Nations as well as the public and the international scientific community, to the greatest extent feasible and practicable, of the nature, conduct, location and results' of space activities.

Value and use of information

But this does not effectively cover the value and use of the information obtained from remote sensing. The distinction between trespass and proprietary rights is vividly expressed in the finding of a US court that the aerial photography of a partly constructed plant, built for the production of methanol by a secret process, was a wrongful appropriation of trade secrets by competitors; but that the flight of the aircraft itself was not a trespass since it was observing federal aviation rules.[4]

The UN General Assembly set up a Working Group in 1971 to consider these and other features of remote sensing, and after making a Report in 1974, the Working Group embodied a number of principles, around which there was consensus, in a draft convention in 1976.[5] But there was a range of opinions and attitudes. At one extreme it was said that remote sensing should be conducted only with the prior consent of the subjacent State (Argentina, Brazil); at the other end the United States maintained not only that remote sensing should be wholly free from control, but that there should be no restrictions on the use of the information obtained, provided that it is made available to all. The draft convention took a middle position, Article 5 (b) stating that:

A State which obtains information concerning natural resources of another State as a result of remote sensing activities shall not be entitled to make it public without the clearly expressed consent of the State, to which the natural resources belong, or to use it in any other

[4] *E. I. du Pont de Nemours* v. *Christopher* [1970] 431 Fed 2nd 1012.
[5] See Maureen Williams, 'Teledetection of Earth Resources from Outer Space', *International Relations* (May 1977), 518.

manner to the detriment of such State. Documentation resulting from remote sensing activities may not be communicated to third parties . . . without the consent of the State whose territory is affected.

It was also generally accepted that States should have access to data available from remote sensing of their territories.

But no convention has yet been adopted on remote sensing and the issue of data distribution is unresolved in form of a general-rule. This is illustrated by the Zaïre–NASA Agreement (1975), which provided for the establishment of a ground station in Zaïre, having access to the Landsat series; but it was an express condition that there should be 'unrestricted public availability' of resource data obtained from the territory of Zaïre. Further, at the Unispace Conference in August 1982 a resolution that States should have the right to veto the distribution of such territorial information was rejected.

World Meteorological Organization

The World Meteorological Organization has a number of programmes of observation of the condition and movements of the atmosphere, using remote sensing by satellites. Its Global Atmospheric Research Programme is divided into a number of projects, for example, on air-ground surface interaction, radiation, including the solar wind, and climate dynamics. Some are geographically oriented, like the Global Atlantic Tropical Experiment, in which ten satellites were operating in 1974.

The environmental effects of space activities are matters of concern. The US National Academy of Sciences observed in 1966 that:

the chemistry of the mesosphere and thermosphere . . . and the processes in those regions that disperse or remove impurities are so little understood. Since rocket activity will increase, and since we are already capable of doubling, in a single year, the quantity of some exotic constituents e.g. atomic sodium, vigorous investigation of aeronomy and high-atmosphere dynamics is a clear pre-requisite to settling the issue of rocket-caused contamination.

The satellite SME (Solar Mesosphere Explorer), designed by the Laboratory of Atmospheric and Space Physics, University of Colorado, to study the creation and distribution of ozone, and launched by NASA also recorded the effects of the eruption of the volcano El Chichon in Mexico in April 1982.

6

Space Stations

Space stations may be of two kinds: a long-life spacecraft, generally geostationary, or an established post or centre on a celestial body. Space stations of the first kind are already being planned, and the established space shuttle is a step towards them. Such stations, in long-life Earth orbit, will have essentially terrestrial functions, as energy plants or factories processing raw materials. At the same time they may be equipped with observation systems, astronomical or strategic and other technical devices, such as for servicing other Earth satellites. Further, these space stations will not only be served by space shuttles, but could be gradually enlarged by materials carried up to them: the possible construction of stations even five kilometres in length is already envisaged. All this will take many years, though the space shuttle has made the initial breakthrough in acting as a carrier vehicle that can attain Earth orbit and then reland as an aircraft. The shuttle may also carry satellites into orbit; and its fuel tanks could be released when empty into a following orbit and be adapted to serve as living quarters.

NASA plans the construction of four more space shuttles by 1986, and the industrial and commercial interest in them is marked. NASA is collaborating with eight aerospace enterprises in production, and Boeing, Transworld Airlines, and Rockwell have all made independent investigations. ESA had undertaken the planning of manned space stations with a number of European enterprises, including British Aerospace; and Eureca, a retrievable satellite, is to be launched for ESA from a US space shuttle in 1986. Spacetron (Space Transportation Service Inc.) of Princeton, New Jersey, is also reported to be seeking the purchase of a space shuttle from NASA to enable it to launch retrievable space vehicles commercially.

The prospect of space stations in orbit, serving as energy plants or as factories processing materials, or even as habitations, is challenging to international law, for it has not yet adapted to the prospect, and it must move forward through the adoption of international conventions, if it is not to be again taken by surprise, as it was when Sputnik went up in 1957.

What then is the status of orbiting space stations, and what regulation of their establishment and use is needed: in particular, is there a common economic interest in them?

Some aid to answering these questions can again be found in the established law of the sea.[1] Is an orbiting space station analogous to a ship or a floating platform? The Outer Space Treaty, Article 8, speaks not of spacecraft or space vehicles but of 'objects' launched into outer space, or landed or constructed on a celestial body, and also of their component parts. Such objects and any 'personnel thereof' remain under the jurisdiction and control of the State on whose registry the object is carried; and the ownership of the object or its component parts is not to be affected by their location, and will be no doubt determinable by rules of private international law. In general then there is some analogy of status as between spacecraft and ships or aircraft.

But many spacecraft, set in geosynchronous orbit, may be described as space stations not least because they are geostationary. Here they critically differ from ships and aircraft. Spatial positions of objects are determined by their relation to chosen reference points. If the centre of the Earth is chosen as reference point, ships, aircraft and spacecraft, when in movement, all change their positions in relation to it in direction and over time. But for the spacecraft in geosynchronous orbit there is a reference point on the surface of the Earth, in perhaps a particular country, in relation to which it is motionless.

In relation then to the surface reference point the spacecraft is stationary, and so can be said to be occupying a place in the sky above that point. Hence the Bogotá Declaration by eight equatorial countries, from Brazil to Indonesia,

[1] For an illuminating study see Kent M. Keith, 'Floating Cities—A New Challenge to Transnational Law', *Marine Policy* (July 1977), 190.

challenging such occupation of places in the sky above their
territories. It is possible that the drafters of Outer Space
Treaty, Article 2, did not envisage an occupation of this kind;
nevertheless the provision, while not apparently excluding
such occupation, is ambiguous about it. It says that it shall
not render the space occupied 'subject to appropriation by
claim of sovereignty'. The State responsible for the operation of the spacecraft would doubtless say that it was not
itself, but the subjacent country, that was making such a
claim. Here some comparison with principles of the exclusive
economic zone, as formulated in the Law of the Sea Convention, is not without interest. We have already referred
briefly to the exclusive economic zone, there are three
notions relevant here: of a defined area of the high seas,
beyond but adjacent to the territorial sea of a coastal State,
an area in which that State has exclusive rights to explore
and exploit the natural resources; of the area being also still
open to all other states for navigation, overflight, and the
laying of cables and pipelines; and of the coastal state having
responsibilities for the conservation and use of the living[2]
resources.

The equatorial belt around the Earth, traversed by geosynchronous spacecraft, can be called an economic zone not
least because it has exceptionally long hours of sunlight, and
thus has a vast natural source of energy from solar radiation,
and because it could be effectively used for the establishment
of space stations. But just as the exclusivity of the marine
economic zone is limited by a number of requirements in the
common interest, there must be analogous requirements in
the exploitation of the equatorial belt of outer space. It has
already had to be recognized that geosynchronous orbits
must not be allowed to become overcrowded; they are a
limited natural resource requiring optimum utilization,
including fair distribution. Estimates vary of the minimum
distance to be kept between satellites in geosynchronous
orbit in order to avoid mutual interference; the number of
satellites that can be maintained simultaneously in orbit must
depend on this. About 100 geosynchronous satellites were in

---

[2] Notably distinguishing them expressly from 'natural resources', which
include oil and minerals.

orbit in 1977 and the number will be more than doubled by 1990. International regulation of the occupation of orbits is plainly necessary.[3]

The conversion of solar radiation into electric power for use on Earth is envisaged, through a network of a large number of geosynchronous space stations, each yielding 5 gigawatts. How then are the economic interests in this energy source to be met? It has first to be asked whether the rule against the appropriation of outer space, in Outer Space Treaty, Article 2, forbids appropriation of its resources. It is plain that, in terms of Article 2, the Sun is a celestial body and that the collection of solar radiation by the means proposed is a use and occupation of outer space. But the question whether that radiation becomes, or can become, the property of operators of the space stations or the States responsible, obviously cannot be resolved by constrictions of Article 2 as it stands. Amendment is necessary.

But an obligation on States responsible for the space stations to distribute the energy derived from them to other countries has a recognizable basis, which perhaps makes the appropriation issue irrelevant. This basis is the politico-legal principle that natural resources, which, like those of the deep sea-bed, the radio spectrum, or outer space, lie beyond the exclusive jurisdiction or control of individual States, are a common province of mankind, to be fairly and efficiently shared. The recognition of rights of land-locked States to a share in marine resources is an illustration of this principle, limited though it is to the living resources. There are of course critical economic factors in the use of space stations as energy plants: the cost, of the capital investment for their construction and of their continued servicing; the choice of recipients and means of distribution of the energy derived; and the various changes to be imposed.

The possibility of space stations being established as factories to process mineral resources obtained from the Moon or other bodies, is at present remote; but the same

[3] S. Gozove, 'The Geosynchronous Orbit: Issues of Law and Policy', 73 *American Journal of International Law* (1979), 444.

economic factors, and particularly the appropriation issue, would come into account, as will be seen below.

The hesitation that surrounds the proposed creation of an international sea-bed authority does not encourage expectation of the creation of such a real authority for the management of space stations and their potential functions.

7

Astronomical Observation

Astronomical observation has, in instrumentation and range, expanded more in this century than in the previous two thousand years. Earth satellites have already made, and will increasingly make, dramatic contributions, and this calls for some attention. In simple terms, astronomy is the scientific study of the solar system, the stars, and galaxies, and quasars, the strangers of the 1960s; while cosmology is the investigation of the large-scale structure of the universe, if indeed it has one. Astronomical observation serves both, and what will be attempted here, in describing the contributions of Earth satellites, is to sketch briefly their enlargements of astronomy, and then to review problems of cosmology, which the satellites may help to solve.

The solar system

Man has walked on the Moon, a step beyond that old hero Columbus, and a camera has stood on Mars, picturing its rock-strewn surface. Of the nine planets revolving around the Sun, a smallish star of middle age, five have now been surveyed,[1] by satellites by photography and other sensors; landings have been made on Venus by USSR spacecraft Venera in 1967 and 1978, and on Mars by US Viking 1 and 2 in 1975 and 1976. Much information has been obtained about their atmospheres, structure, and geological composition. The search for life on Mars has revealed nothing so far in the form of biological traces, though the research by Viking 1 and 2 was of course very limited in range.

As far as mineral resources go, samples of Moon rock and soil have been brought back to Earth for investigation, and

---

[1] A comprehensive survey of their exploration, with outstanding photographs, is Peter Francis, *The Planets* (Penguin, 1981).

some on-the-spot analysis was carried out by Viking 1 and 2
on Mars. But neither tests disclosed the presence of either
novel or plentiful minerals. How far then either body can be
a source of minerals needed on Earth will depend on further
exploration, and on a decision as to whether extraction can
be economic. Many techniques are possible: the separation
of Moon soils into oxides and metals, and the combination
of fusion of raw materials.[2] The possible role of space stations
has already been described.

The outer planets are not only at great distances—it took
Voyager 2 almost five years to reach Saturn, a period including a survey of Jupiter—but their atmospheric and
surface conditions make satellite landings doubtful. Nevertheless remarkable photographs have been obtained by satellite
of Jupiter and Saturn and some fascinating discoveries have
been made: for example, that Jupiter and Uranus both have
encircling rings though smaller in width than those of Saturn,
and that Io, one of Jupiter's four larger moons, has active
volcanoes. Indeed it is perhaps the moons of the large planets
that call for further investigation. There is speculation that
Europa, another of Jupiter's larger moons, which has most
of its surface covered by water-ice, may have sufficient
induced heating in its interior, in part by radioactive elements,
to melt the lower level of the ice and so provide the needed
conditions for primitive life.

The Draft Agreement on the Activities of States on the
Moon and Other Celestial Bodies, adopted by General
Assembly Resolution 34/68 (5 December 1979), has much to
say about solar system operations: it lays down three principles. First, the natural resources of the Moon are 'the
common heritage of mankind' and the use of the Moon shall
be carried out 'for the benefit and in the interests of all
countries, irrespective of their degree of economic or scientific development' (Articles 11 (i) and 4 (i)). These provisions
follow almost verbatim provisions of the Outer Space Treaty.
Secondly, 'Neither the surface nor the subsurface of the
Moon, nor any part thereof or natural resources in place'
shall become the property of any State, organization, or legal
or natural person (Article 11 (3)); however, samples of

[2] D. Griswell and P. Marsh, 'Working on the Moon', *New Scientist* (1.10.1981).

minerals and other substances may be collected and removed from the Moon, and shall 'remain at the disposal' of the States responsible to be used for 'scientific purposes' (Article 6 (2)). Thirdly, the States parties to the Agreement undertake to establish an international regime 'to govern the exploitation of the natural resources' of the Moon when that becomes feasible (Article 11 (5)). The main purposes are the orderly and rational development and management of the natural resources and 'an equitable sharing by all States parties in the benefits derived', special considerations being given to the interests and needs of the developing countries, and to the efforts of countries that have contributed to the exploration of the Moon (Article 11 (7)).

These provisions are less clear on property rights to the resources than those analogous provisions of the Law of the Sea Convention, already described, relating to the resources of the deep sea-bed. In fact, there appears to be a careful avoidance of the issue. But a natural explanation which is perhaps the most likely, is that this whole problem of transfer to Earth of Moon resources, and possibly of resources obtained from other bodies, and of the economic rights and interests in them, was left to be resolved in the international regime, to be established when the exploitation of these resources becomes a reality.

How far the exploration of the solar system, and particularly of the Moon and Mars, will continue must depend in great part on finance. Satellite missions, specifically designed for such exploration, may be reduced in the coming years in budget cuts.

A monitoring system, placed on the Moon in 1969, was closed down in 1979 for lack of maintenance funds, though it was still operating effectively. The US Office of Management and Budget also called for reductions in space expenditure from the end of 1981: in particular by way of a 'turn-off' of Voyager 2, due to pass Uranus in 1986 and Neptune in 1989, and the abandonment by NASA of a project to send a satellite to Jupiter to enter its atmosphere and to make further study of its moons. NASA has cancelled the probe of Halley's Comet, due in 1986, and a planned orbiting radar of Venus, and has also withdrawn from the

International Solar Polar Mission. The ESA however plans a satellite named Giotto, to survey Halley's Comet, and also probes which will examine various planets. The cost of installing equipment to extract and dispose of mineral resources on the Moon, let alone Mars, even if it could be shown that the operation was worth it in economic terms to meet needs of energy or industrial materials, would be enormous.

Beyond the solar system

Astronomy differs from many sciences in having no physical or experimental contact with its objects in order to determine their nature, at any rate where they are located beyond the solar system. It depends wholly upon observation, and up to the last half-century largely on eye, telescope, and camera. But gradually the electromagnetic spectrum has been opened up beyond the visible bands, as a means of observation, and Earth satellites are particularly well fitted to this kind of observation; and much of their work is directed outside the solar system. The contribution they have made, and will make to observation beyond the solar system, is so great and even dramatic that it demands some description.

Orbiting satellites, such as Uhuru, launched from Kenya in 1970, and Heaoz (Einstein), active from 1978 to 1981, and satellites now planned, can vastly extend observation by avoiding atmospheric absorption. At present operating[3] are IUE (International Ultraviolet Explorer) carrying a 45 cm reflecting telescope, launched by ESA with the co-operation of the US and the UK; two Japanese satellites Hakudo, launched in 1979, and Tenma (Astrob), launched in February 1983, both carrying X-ray detectors; and IRAS (Infra-red Astronomical Satellite) designed to survey the whole sky for detection of infra-red sources, and launched in January 1983 by the US, the Netherlands, and the UK in co-operation. In April 1983 the USSR launched the largest space telescope to be placed in Earth orbit, having a mirror 3.8 m in diameter. Its ellipitcal orbit is itself enormous, the satellite carrying the telescope being at its furthest point nearly half-way to the Moon. A number of similar detector

[3] Described in *New Scientist* (31.3.1983).

Box 6

The range of electromagnetic radiation covered in astronomical observation may be briefly presented with wavelengths in metres

Cosmic ray background	Gamma rays	X-rays	Ultra-violet (visible)	Infra-red	Radio waves
10^{-17}	10^{-13}	10^{-11}	10^{-7}	10^{-6}	10^{-3}

Energy and temperature of objects observed increase generally as wavelength diminishes, but there are many different sources of radiation in one body. *Radio Sources, infra-red and ultraviolet radiation, X-rays, and gamma rays* provide much information about the physical structure, behaviour, and evolution of stars and galaxies, and the range and composition of interstellar dust-clouds and other material. The background of *cosmic radiation* is similar in source temperature and character and comes from all directions; this isotropic feature of it suggests a symmetric universe.

Radio waves and the larger infra-red waves pass through to the surface of the Earth without interference; but, from the shorter infra-red waves, through the narrow band of the visible spectrum, into the larger ultraviolet waves, there is a selective absorption of radiation by atmosphere; and shorter ultraviolet waves and X-rays are wholly absorbed.

satellites are planned by the USSR—two of them in collaboration with France—the US, the Federal Republic of Germany, and ESA, for launching up to 1986.

The increased range of radiation open to astronomical observation also reflects the union of astronomy and physics. For example, the energy output, atomic patterns, metallic content, of stars; the related structure and history of our own and the external galaxies; and the role in all of gravitation and other forces are being intensely and fruitfully studied. Dennis Sciama has said:[4]

The exploration of the Universe, as conducted by physicists, astronomers, and cosmologists, is one of the greatest intellectual adventures of

[4] D. W. Sciama, *Modern Cosmology* (Cambridge University Press, 1971), p. vii.

the mid-twentieth century . . . their achievements, especially in the last few years, constitute a revolution in our knowledge and understanding of the Universe without parallel in the recorded history of mankind.

The understanding of the universe is as exciting as it is difficult, and another leading cosmologist has said of the Space Telescope planned for launching in 1985:[5]

By enabling astronauts to observe objects up to 50 times fainter than hitherto possible with ground-based instruments this telescope is expected to improve and enlarge our understanding of the extragalactic world. Astrophysicists of to-day who hold the view that 'the ultimate cosmological problem' has been more or less solved will be in for a few surprises before this century runs out.

Cosmology

A bold attempt may then be made here to review the state of contemporary cosmology and to describe some of the uncertainties that Earth satellites can help to resolve.

Given the notion of the universe as the totality of what is or can be observed, it is pictured as perhaps limitless space containing units of matter that are evolving over time. The main role of astronomical satellites is to extend dramatically that observation. For centuries, the observed universe has been confined to our solar system—the Sun, planetary bodies, and comets—and the stars and hazy patches of light called nebulae; and although Kant, in the early stages of his thinking, had speculated about the possibility of separate systems, island universes as he called them, he abandoned the idea. The Milky Way and the constellations were not seen as constituting a system, though the Milky Way is 'powdered with stars': Galileo so described it in 1638 in a meeting in Florence with John Milton, who was on a European tour, having met Grotius in Paris. However, the nebulae remained a puzzle and were ultimately to be seen as 'islands', though not universes. The French astronomer, Charles Messier (1730–1817), working at the Marine Observatory at Cluny, focused his attention on comets, of which he discovered thirteen, and Louis XV called him the ferret of comets. But he was struck by the optical similarities and obvious

[5] Jayant Narlikar, 'Was there a big bang?', *New Scientist* (2.7.1981), 19.

differences between comets and nebulae, and he made a catalogue of the latter listing 103. It was published in 1784, and it included what are now known to be gas clouds and globular star clusters within our galaxy, as well as many external galaxies.[6] William Herschel expressed the belief in 1811 that some at least of the Messier objects were beyond the Milky Way and the constellations; but more than a century was to pass before a means of distance measurement was found to demonstrate their separation.

In 1922 Edwin Hubble, operating the 100-inch reflector telescope at Mount Wilson in California, then the largest telescope in the world, made the great breakthrough. He found not only that M31, the Great Nebula in Andromeda, as it was historically called, was similar in structure and composition to the Milky Way system, but he identified certain stars in it, whose known characteristics made the determination of their distance possible. The distance of M31 was finally established at about 2.2 million light-years, a scale of distance far beyond any yet imagined. It then became clear that the Milky Way system and M31 were separate galaxies.

Galaxies are individual systems and are composed of stars and clusters of stars, and masses of interstellar gas and dust. They vary greatly in size and structure, and are classified largely according to shape: elliptical; spiral and barred spiral; irregular. Their evolution and age appear related to structure, elliptical galaxies being on one view at the earlier stage. Our galaxy—the Milky Way system—is a spiral, in shape not unlike a fried egg, being a broadly circular, flattish system, denser in the middle regions. The diameter of the galaxy is about 100,000 light-years and the solar system lies 30,000 light-years from its centre. There are many groups or clusters of galaxies; and what is known as the Local Group is composed of M31 and our galaxy, and fifteen other galaxies, all much smaller. The scale of distances between galaxies and their measurement raise still unsolved problems of observation and cosmology, and Earth satellites can contribute to solutions.

---

[6] Kenneth Glyn-Jones, *Messier's Nebulae and Star Clusters* (Faber and Faber, 1968), p. 23. This superb volume contains the famous Messier catalogue, complete with photographs, sky diagrams, and a wealth of technical and informative materials. The numbering of the objects 'M1 to M103' is still used.

Box 7

Astronomical distance measurements may be briefly described.

Local distances, including the nearer stars, are measured by the *parallax* method. Hold a finger upright in line with a distant lamp-post; close the left eye and the finger will appear to the right of the post, close the right eye and the finger will appear to the left of the post, the line between the eyes subtending an angle at the finger. Now take the positions of the Earth in orbit around the Sun at an interval of six months. In this rough diagram—

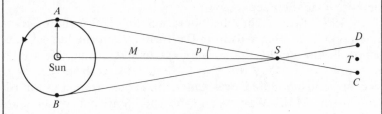

the distances are of course far greater and the angles smaller than represented—if A is the first position of the Earth (left eye) and B the position six months later (right eye), then a nearby star S will appear in relation to a remote[7] star T (the lamp-post) at C (left-eye view) and D (right-eye view). The angle at S subtending the radius of the orbit of the Earth—its distance from the Sun R —is half the angle subtending the distance between A and B, and is the *parallax* (p). Since R is known (149,600,000 km) the distance of the Star can be determined by trigonometry.[8] A parallax of one second of arc called a *parsec* would represent a distance of 30.872×10^{12} km.

A *light-year* is the distance travelled by light in one year and is the basic unit of measurement of astronomical distances. Using approximate figures, we have 300,000 km per second as the constant velocity of light, so that one light-year is about 9.46×10^{12} km and 1 parsec = 3.26 light-years. The parallax of the nearest observed star is 0.754 seconds of arc, so that its distance is $1/p$ or about 4.32 light-years.

Returning to space travel, a spacecraft attaining a speed of 72,000 km per hour would take over 60,000 years to reach it; and even if it could approach the speed of light with a relativistic time reduction for the occupants, their journey would still take many years.

---

[7] Its relative remoteness will be estimated by its magnitude and other means.

[8] Since p is so small the distances of the star from the Earth and the Sun can be treated as almost equivalent, and the trigonometry—$1/p$.

The identification of particular kinds of star in a galaxy enables its distance to be measured, if the luminosity of that kind of star is known; for, since there is a direct relation between the observed brightness and distance of an object —the further away, the fainter it is—the distance of a star can be derived if its real luminosity is known and its observed brightness measured, called respectively its absolute magnitude and apparent magnitude. The approximate distances of the nearer galaxies can be determined in this way, though not without some margin of error, depending on the precision of the various observations involved; and the distance of the cluster of galaxies nearest to the Local Group is estimated at between forty and fifty million light-years.

But this is about the limit of possible identification of stars in a galaxy by telescopic photography, since beyond it a galaxy is visually very small. However, the spectra of stars, and of distant galaxies, are also basic means of observation; and particular forms of radiation, as recorded, may lead to the identification of certain stars as present in a galaxy, and, if their character is known, the distance may still be assessed.

The luminosity–distance ratio, already described, may also be applied to galaxies. So the observed size and luminosity of an elliptical galaxy situated in the neighbouring cluster at approximately forty million light-years distance can be used as the base for measuring the distances of similar galaxies, progressively smaller in their observed size and luminosity; the distances of two galaxies, visually star like objects, have been assessed at about 1.3 billion and 1.9 billion light-years respectively. But there are complications, which make such measurements at best rough approximations with margins of error of 20 per cent or more; the inherent luminosity naturally varies with the actual size and structure of the galaxy, and precise measurement of the observed size and luminosity becomes increasingly difficult with faint, small objects. Here Earth-satellite telescopes will help.

In 1929 Slipher in the United States found, in the examination of the spectra of forty galaxies, that in almost all of them there were shifts of the spectral lines from their normal, laboratory positions towards the longer wavelength, lower frequency, 'redder' end of the spectrum. This came to be called the red-shift, and its interpretation, still largely maintained, was that it was a Doppler effect. This, demonstrated by C. J. Doppler (1803-53), is a change in the frequency and wavelength of sound, or electromagnetic radiation, due to relative motion of the source and the observer. The pitch or frequency of an approaching source is higher, and its wavelength is shortened, in effect by the movement (a blue-shift in the spectrum), whereas, if the source is receding the frequency is observed as diminishing and the wavelength increasing (red-shift). The similar sound effect of a passing ambulance blowing its horn is familiar.

If the red-shift is a Doppler effect then the galaxies are in recession; and even with the great increase in the number of galaxies observed, there was no exception, save for a few understood cases, in any direction; all galaxies showed redshifts in their spectra. But since the Earth is not a centre from which galaxies can be receding—an observer in a distant galaxy would see our galaxy, with the Earth in it, as also receding—space as a whole must be expanding. A simple illustration is spots on an air balloon; as the balloon expands, the spots move apart.

In a further analysis of spectral lines Hubble found that the size of the red-shift was proportional to the estimated distance of the galaxy; in other words, the greater the distance of a galaxy, the more rapid is its recession[9] and so the expansion of space was more rapid at earlier times. This follows from the fact that, given the time taken for light or other radiation to reach us from a galaxy, we are seeing it as it was perhaps one billion years ago.

But the general theory of relativity had brought critical changes in traditional, supposedly natural, ways of thinking about space, time, and matter. Confirmed by observational tests, the theory states that neither space nor time have on the large scale absolute linear dimensions. Space is subject to distortion by concentrations of matter in it, and gravitation is not an independent force but a physical effect of the distortion of space, which may, on a large scale, be a kind

[9] This Hubble Constant is now estimated to be around 50 km per second per megaparsec (3,260,000 light-years) though, as will be seen, this is reduced by some experts.

of curvature: so a galaxy has been found by what is called a 'gravitational lens' to create a double image of an object far more distant but visually close to it. Further, the time-scale of a concentration of matter may vary with the velocity at which it moves in space.

A contemporary and widely accepted model of the universe has three parts: that it is expanding; that going back in time, the expansion began with an explosion of energy—the 'big bang'; and that the universe is homogeneous and isotropic, that is to say that it is broadly the same in structure and composition in whatever direction, or from whatever position it is observed, though this does not exclude clusters and superclusters of galaxies.

The evidence of expansion of the observed universe is strong, based on the red-shift as an indicator of recession, but there are difficulties in the measurement of this expansion. Here the identification of quasars in 1963 was a dramatic development. Called quas(i-stell)ar because, like stars, they were small points of visible radiation, they had extraordinary features. They are shown to be relatively small in size—some no bigger than the solar system—and yet to radiate energy on a level comparable to that of a whole galaxy. Further, if their red-shifts are a measure of distance, they range from, for example, a red-shift of 0.16 representing a distance of about 2 billion light-years to 3.53, which would indicate a distance around 12 billion light-years. Since over twenty years no more distant object has been observed, are we here at the frontier of space, and in time, looking back at objects near the 'beginning' of the universe? These remote quasars would in fact be primitive galaxies.

We come then to the second feature of the 'big bang', the explosion initiating the expansion. At least two doubts arise about it. First, if the distances given above are reliable, the evolution of the most remote primitive galaxy would have taken a considerable time to reach its observed state and the estimated 'age' of the universe would be about 15 billion years. But it is asked whether the scale of red-shifts is wholly reliable: some quasars have been observed close to, and even physically related to, more developed galaxies, the red-shifts of quasars and galaxy being different. Further, the size of the Hubble Constant of recession has been questioned and reduced: a resulting 'age' of the universe would then be 10 billion years.

The second doubt about the 'big bang' is more conceptional. It was, as conceived, a singularity, a material condition or event without cause or explanation. Yet the physical description of it—the emergence of matter in subatomic form in the first tiny fraction of a second followed in minutes by the development of hydrogen atoms—assumes a causal process. We have then a causeless cause.

The 'steady state' model of the universe in part avoids this contradiction. Pleading a 'perfect cosmological principle', this maintains that the universe, being homogeneous and isotropic, does not undergo, and has never undergone, any major changes, and had no beginning. In the words of John Taylor: 'The universe has no meaning, no purpose; it just is, as energy.' But this model has still to take account of the evidence of expansion; for there cannot be both continuous space expansion, and separation of matter within it, and at the same time the maintenance of uniform density in a 'steady state'. It is therefore suggested that hydrogen atoms emerge out of nothing, in minute numbers over vast periods of time, but sufficient to maintain density: in other words, there is a kind of continuous beginning.

The 'big bang' model is presently preferred, but it is then asked whether expansion of space continues indefinitely, whether the universe is 'open'; or whether the density of matter is sufficient to bring expansion to a halt by gravitational effects, leading to a reverse contraction, and perhaps a new 'big bang'—a cyclical universe.

Earth satellites will contribute much to the answering of some of these vast questions. They are carrying large telescopes, which have a far greater range of vision, not being confined by the Earth's atmosphere;[10] but also, by recording radiation outside the visible range they are providing extensive new information, not least in the areas described above.

[10] This is overcome in part by the telescopes recently established on mountain peaks at Las Palmas in the Canaries. The US space shuttle is to carry a telescope with a mirror 2.4 m in diameter, almost the size of the 100-inch telescope at Mount Wilson. Refined estimates of stellar distances can also be made by Hipparcos (High Precision Parallax collecting Satellites), organized by ESA.

The High Energy Astronomical Observatory, launched by NASA in 1979, was a high-resolution X-ray telescope. X-ray emissions from high-energy sources were recorded by it—exploding stars and the nuclei of galaxies—and were the only radiation received from quasars. The emissions reveal the ionized state of many metals, including iron, magnesium, and calcium; and so deduction can be made as to the structure and age of stars and gas clouds, from which the X-rays come. British X-ray detectors had been carried in satellites in 1972; and Exosat, launched by the European Space Agency on Ariane in November 1981, is to be followed in 1987 by more elaborate detectors in an ESA satellite and the Japanese Astro-C, which will carry a British detector.

IRAS (Infra-red Radiation Satellite) was constructed and programmed by physicists and engineers in the US, the Netherlands, and the United Kingdom, working in combination. Launched in January 1983, after some preliminary difficulties, to be in polar orbit at an altitude of 900 km for about a year, it has already yielded outstanding information from the infra-red sky.[11] Turning back to the problem of the density of matter in space, it may be noted that it is assumed that physical laws and constants—the mass of elementary particles, gravity, nuclear forces, and their relationships—are homogeneous over time; this assumption is supported by the fact that spectral lines emitted from remote objects billions of years ago are in a recognizable standard form.

Calculations indicate that if the density of matter in observed space, measured as mass divided by volume, is greater than unity, the universe would appear to be 'open'; but if it is less than unity the universe is 'closed' undergoing an ultimate contraction. It is interesting here that the kind of universe we have falls within fairly narrow limits of density of matter, gravity, and nuclear forces. If, for example, nuclear forces were slightly weaker, no chemical elements more complex than hydrogen could be stable; if slightly stronger, the physical evolution of matter and the stars would be wholly different from what it is. Again, if gravitation were weaker the expansion of space would be more rapid, limiting

[11] From relative cool bodies, such as gas-clouds and even solar systems.

and reducing the condensation of matter; if stronger, expansion would be on a smaller scale and stars would be smaller with shorter lives. The current estimates of the density of matter place it at less than 0.5 of the mass divided by the volume of observed space:[12] in short, the universe is 'open', a one-off job.

IRAS may be bringing hesitation to this conclusion. It has already observed matter in space, previously unknown, in the forms of three more rings of dust and gas around the solar system, and of over one hundred low-temperature point-like objects, the distance and nature of which remain unknown, and of interstellar clouds of dust and gas.

Black holes, already theoretically conceived with also some faint observational evidence, may be identified by satellites[13] and if there are great numbers of them, the density of matter could be increased.

Satellites too will make possible the determination of a frontier of space, if there is one. If present distance measurements can be maintained with perhaps some modifications, and no objects are found beyond around 12 billion light-years, that could be a limit of space and time, decisive for an understanding of the character of the universe.

Earth satellites promise an enlargement of astronomical knowledge on a scale without precedent in history.

In conclusion, some words of the great Stephen Hawking may be recalled:

The more we examine the universe, we find it is not arbitrary, but obeys certain well-defined laws that operate in different areas. It seems very reasonable to suppose that there may be some unifying principles, so that all laws are part of some bigger laws.

---

[12] It is averaged out at about 10^{-30} grams per cubic centimetre, or the equivalent of one hydrogen atom in a cubic metre. This is a density less than that in a laboratory vacuum container in which some particles of air survive.

[13] The satellite named International Ultraviolet Explorer (IUE), a US, UK, and ESA project operating since 1978, has revealed what is believed to be a black hole in a galaxy of a familiar type at a distance of 50 million light years. Gamma-ray sources are also centres of universe power, including black holes: their study was pioneered by the US Satellite SAS-2 (1972-3) and the European satellite CO5-B (1975-82), and will be developed by the US Gamma-ray Observatory to be launched towards the end of the 1980s.

In a similar spirit Einstein once remarked that what is incomprehensible about the universe is that it is comprehensible.

8

Strategic Uses of Outer Space

We return now to Earth and to grimmer prospects. It is well-known that, in the use of spacecraft, a large part of the expenditure and development of technology in both the USSR and the United States is directed to military objectives. Strategic uses of Earth satellites may be understood to include weaponry, surveillance, and counteraction against missiles and satellites.

Weaponry

In a statement by the United States Senate in May 1980 it was said that:

Space systems provide critical strategic and tactical support to military forces and political leaders in the areas of attack, warning, navigation, surveillance, communications, intelligence and meteorology.

The statement is not confined to technology; for, in the reference to tactical support for political leaders, there is implied their ambivalent attitudes to attack and defence. To avoid charges of having aggressive policies, political leaders habitually use the language of defence and deterrence. Space developments help to persuade the public both that the threat of attack from the other side is growing, and that technology must be directed to the expansion of defence, providing means of counter-attack or even a first strike, as a consequent warning and deterrent to the other side.

Technology is dominant. In face of the production and use of armaments national social choices have given way to a 'primitive will to survive' and, to borrow a Darwinian idea, advanced social man has become an instrument of technological selection. Unrestricted technology produces the 'force multipliers', which constantly destabilize arms parity as a political objective; and the fittest to survive become those selected by the technological advances.

The influence of technological advances, determinant of industrial and strategic policy, is illustrated not only by the development of outer space weaponry itself, but also by the invention and testing of anti-satellite devices and other means of counteraction. Already an imbalance is appearing between weapon capacity and the potentialities of counteraction. The United States Defense Guidance instrument, directed to a five-year strategic plan, states that:

The US Space Program will contribute to the deterrence of an attack on the US, or, if deterrence fails, to the prosecution of war by developing, deploying, and operating support space systems.

It follows that it is necessary 'to deny the enemy the use of his space systems that are harmful to our efforts during conflict', and so:

We must insure that treaties and agreements do not foreclose opportunities to develop these capabilities. In particular it must be recognized that agreements cannot protect our defense interests in space during periods of hostilities.

These reservations made about international agreements will be considered later, and it is enough here to point to the anxiety expressed in this statement on Defense Guidance about the growing efficiency of anti-satellite devices.

Let us see first some of the weapons. An extreme, remote, and novel kind of weapon would be a nuclear explosion detonated at an altitude of perhaps 70 miles, just on the edge of outer space, which would generate electromagnetic impulses. These would penetrate the atmosphere, and could interrupt or jam all radio-communications within an area of around 600 square miles: in effect, all operational radio-communications of the armed services could be put out of action for a considerable time. But, as often, there could be obstacles to this kind of operation; for, while microchips are said to be more vulnerable to electromagnetic impulses than the older type of valves, fibre optics as a vehicle of light pulses could be immune, and their increasing use is well known.

Outer space weaponry has generally a number of forms: for

example, missiles and instruments of missile guidance carried in orbit; anti-satellite devices, including laser and particle-team transmitters; and missiles stored in space stations.

Ballistic missiles, travelling from ground to ground by parabolic flight, are guided only in the initial stages of their flight. Fractional orbital ballistic missiles (FOBS), which are, as described in SALT II documents, 'weapons of mass destruction', and are capable of traversing part of an Earth orbit, are nevertheless without directional control in the later stages of flight; and ICBMs (Inter-continental ballistic missiles) have the further disadvantage of having fixed immobile ground bases.

Cruise missiles have two advantages over these earlier systems: they can fly at low altitudes, making detection and the needed rapid intervention in defence very difficult; further, they can be redirected during flight by satellites. They are carried into operation by large aircraft, each containing twelve missiles, a cargo of sixteen or more being planned. The Cruise missile is a formidable weapon, having a thermonuclear warhead with the explosive force of about 200,000 tonnes of TNT, or more than ten times that of the Hiroshima bomb. It is designed to adapt its flight level from 15 m over flat country to 50 m over undulating land and 100 m over mountains, using 'terrain and contour matching' (TERCOM), provided by detailed maps derived from satellite reconnaissance photographs and computer storage of altitudes. Further satellite guidance can bring the missile within 30 m of its target. The average speed of a Cruise missile is about 800 km per hour, and its range is around 2,500 km, roughly the distance from Paris to Moscow.

A comparison of the Cruise missile with the USSR's SS 20, a ballistic missile replacing a series of earlier weapons, and endowed with a far higher degree of accuracy than those, shows that each of these ballistic missiles has some superiority over the other. The SS 20 has a range of 3,500–4,000 km, making it usable in wider geographical contexts than the Cruise missile. But its destructive potential is less: it has three independently guided thermonuclear warheads; each having an explosive force of 15,000 tonnes of TNT. The Cruise missiles carried by one B52 would then have an explosive force equivalent to five SS 20s; and after release they would be capable of hitting more targets.

Weapon guidance will be developed in the US Navstar system in the late 1980s. Designed both for position finding and tactical weapon guidance, the system will have eight satellites in three circular orbits, and methods of overcoming electronic interference with guidance are being sought.

The control or domination of weapons in outer space has made no progress. The USSR submitted a draft convention to the UN in 1981, of which the prime provision was:

States parties undertake not to place in orbit around the Earth objects carrying weapons of any kind, install such weapons on celestial bodies, or station such weapons in outer space in any other manner, including stationing on reusable manned space vehicles of an existing type, or of other types which States parties may develop in the future (Article 1 (1)).

The Unispace conclusions in August 1982, adopted by ninety-four countries, went no further than calling for a specific ban on 'testing, stationing and deployment of any weapons in space'. Neither formulation, even if adopted, would cover the guidance of missiles to precise targets by a navigation satellite. However, both go some way to clarifying the provisions of the Outer Space Treaty (1967).

The Outer Space Treaty (1967) is concerned with two aspects of the military uses of outer space: directly, in prohibiting the placement in orbit or otherwise in outer space, or on celestial bodies, of 'nuclear weapons or other kinds of weapons of mass destruction' (Article IV), and indirectly, in requiring preliminary consultation before any activity or experiment is undertaken, which may 'cause potentially harmful interference with activities of other States Parties in the peaceful exploration and use of outer space' (Article IX). The ambiguity of 'peaceful' is well known. Does it mean non-military or simply non-aggressive? The addition of 'purposes' in Article IV brings in the notions both of intent and of consequences: the activity must not be designed to terminate in some use of force contrary to international law. The terms of Articles IV and IX fail to recognize the mixed character of spacecraft and of space operations. Its last two sentences allow, first, the use of military personnel for 'scientific research or for any other peaceful purposes', and, more remarkably, the use of 'any equipment of facility' for the 'peaceful exploration' of celestial bodies. A manned Earth satellite may then engage both in remote sensing and surveillance, which, it would then be argued, is 'peaceful' in that it is not designed to attack, and may even be a new way of maintaining peace—an Outer Space Treaty objective —by stabilizing the relations of armed powers. But can the stationing of a navigation satellite capable of guiding a missile to its target be a 'peaceful' activity? Is it not in fact an operative part of a 'weapon'? The possibility of inspection of installations and equipment placed on celestial bodies is limited by the condition of reciprocity in Article XII; but in the next decades the number of countries engaged in space operations on this scale is unlikely to increase to the extent that reciprocity can be an effective condition between more than a few countries.

Surveillance

There is, however, something positive in the development of surveillance by satellite. Similar to remote sensing, it provides the inspection and ratification of military activities which were missing in the older attempts at disarmament. The US launched its first surveillance satellite Samos 2 in 1961 and by 1973 109 satellites had mapped most areas of military interest. A recently established satellite, KHII, is in orbit for two years. There can be few military zones, installations of even small size, and movements, which are not known and detectable in any part of the globe; even nuclear-powered submarines may be 'seen'.

Earth satellites have the advantage that their wide-ranging functions can be mixed. A satellite may be designed and function as a channel for telecommunications or remote sensing or astronomical observation, but some of the mechanisms may also be convertible to military uses, or both kinds of mechanism may be carried; and it is not easy to infer from the style and behaviour of a satellite, and its chosen orbit, what function it is performing, though the choice of a relatively low altitude orbit may be an indicator.[1] The dual use of an observation technique is illustrated by the detection of infra-red radiation from heat sources; volcanic activity is detected by Landsat and SPOT; nuclear explosions in outer space by VELA, a US satellite, two of which operate at a distance of 60,000 miles.

The modes of satellite surveillance are mainly photographic and electronic. Photographic reconnaissance of land areas is carried out, for example, by the US air force, some USSR Cosmos satellites and Salyut 3 and 5, and by China 7, launched in 1976. Electronic reconnaissance takes place of air-defence and missile-defence radar systems, the location of which can be pin-pointed.[2] Similar detection of ship-borne radar and communication signals is also effective; and the movement of nuclear submarines can be identified by infra-red detection of the water used to cool the reactor, which is expelled as heated into the sea. Infra-red sensors of the hot 'plume' of a launched rocket, or missile engine, and of nuclear radiation, can also operate as early-warning devices; the US VELA satellites, orbiting at an altitude of 90,000 km, can detect nuclear detonation. The US Defence Satellite Communications system operates through four satellites, connecting twenty-seven command centres. Voice and teletype messages and images, and computerized data, can be carried, and mobile ground-stations are used.

As regards the international attempts at regulation of surveillance, the Anti-Ballistic Missile Treaty (1972) provided that:

each Party shall use national technical means of verification at its disposal in a manner consistent with generally recognised principles of international law . . . Each Party undertakes not to inferfere with the national technical means of verification of the other Party.

ABM radars were also not to exceed specified numbers.

Both the UN and the European Parliament have proposed the creation of an international surveillance agency. The

---

[1] US satellites LASP and Big Bird (air force reconnaissance) and KHII, and some USSR Cosmos satellites, engaged in surveillance, are in orbits below 500 km altitude.

[2] A satellite planned for 1987–90 will be composed of seven geosynchronous and four polar satellites, and will include electronic sensors to detect anti-satellite weapons.

possible monitoring, which the agency might conduct, would include coverage of the military use of chemicals and bacteria, and military border movements. The US and USSR have both opposed such an agency.

General inspection of space activities was envisaged in UN General Assembly Resolution 1148-XII (14 November 1957), which called for:

Joint study of an inspection system designed to ensure that the sending of objects through outer space shall be exclusively for peaceful and scientific purposes.

The Outer Space Treaty makes modest provision for the inspection of spacecraft in transit or in Earth orbit, States parties 'shall consider on a basis of equality' requests to 'observe the flight' of spacecraft by other States parties. Observation, which is itself not defined, depends on agreement as to its nature and conditions (Article 10). However, stations, installations, equipment, and space vehicles, on the Moon, or other celestial bodies, shall be 'open' to representatives of other States parties, 'on a basis of reciprocity'. Reciprocity appears to differ subtly from equality, for presumably a State party, which had itself not placed any stations and so on on site, could not claim a right of inspection. However, the Moon Agreement resolves the difference by providing in Article 15 (1) that:

Each State may assure itself that the activities of other States parties in the exploration and use of the Moon are compatible with the provisions of this Agreement. To that end, all space vehicles, equipment, facilities, stations and installations, shall be open to other States parties.

In pursuance of such an inspection, a State party may seek assistance from the UN.

Counteraction against satellites

But it is anti-satellite devices, that are occupying much current attention and activity, not least because they are upsetting whatever balance there may have been reached in outer space weaponry; and there is then the 'destabilization' characteristic of the arms race. The devices under development, or already constructed, range from instruments of destruction to interference.

Apart from ground-based anti-satellite missiles or lasers, satellites themselves may be manœuvrable, and thus can be exploded on command to destroy another satellite; and space shuttles in orbit could be used to inspect and if necessary capture satellites, but it would need either a space station to house it, or doors and compartments in the space shuttle large enough to take it.

The US made a destructor satellite operational in 1979. It was designed to intercept its satellite target, when its cargo of explosives would be detonated, but it was at this first stage limited to low-orbit targets.

Lasers[3] are a means of intercepting objects travelling through outer space by 'blinding' their sensors or even injuring them to the point of putting them out of action. So, depending on its power, the laser beams may interrupt guidance signals sent to a satellite, or disrupt its sensors, or even pierce its aluminium skin, this last stroke being also capable of use against missiles.

The Nuclear Test Ban Treaty (1963), described as partial because it is directed primarily to environmental protection —it does not exclude underground explosions—provides that:

Each of the Parties to this Treaty undertakes to prohibit, to prevent, and not to carry out, any nuclear weapon test explosion, or any other nuclear explosion, at any place under its jurisdiction or control:
(a) in the atmosphere; beyond its limits, including outer space; or under water, including territorial waters or high seas.

This would appear to prohibit the use of a nuclear explosive to destroy a satellite in orbit, but the Treaty has an important limitation. While it is expressed to be of unlimited duration, a party to it has 'the right to withdraw from the Treaty if it decides that extraordinary events, related to the subject matter of this Treaty', have jeopardized the supreme interests of 'its country' (Article IV). Not only is this a large qualification, making possible the use, already

---

[3] Light amplification by stimulated emission of radiation. Lasers vary in composition and wavelength, which determine the degree of atmospheric absorption and beam strength.

described, of a nuclear explosion in outer space to put military communications out of action; but China and France did not become parties to the Treaty, and between 1963 and 1977 China conducted nineteen and France forty-one atmospheric nuclear explosions, though their altitude is not reported.[4]

[4] *Arms Control: Survey and Appraisal of Multinational Agreements* (Stockholm International Peace Research Institute, 1978), Appendix D.

A General View

Predictions would be rash but some observations may be made on the basis of the influences that appear to be at work in space activities.

It has been well said that many of the attributes of contemporary man, that have enabled him to survive and to dominate other creatures and displace weaker races, are now out of place, being 'exactly the opposite of what is required to provide him with the wisdom he so desperately needs for the harmonious development of human society'; and the necessities of a world watch on ecological dangers, disarmament, increased food production, and the development of new energy sources, are demonstrated.

Space technology and operations are ambivalent precisely because they not only express these attributes of contemporary man that are now out of place, but also provide the needed world-watch; they both aggravate some international problems and provide solutions for others. After a brief review of space operations and international action concerning them, we may draw attention to some of the principal influences: strategic issues; the costing and choice of space programmes; the role of private enterprise; and attitudes to space activities in the Third World.

The historic launch of Sputnik I from the USSR on 4 October 1957, was followed by the launch of the first telecommunications satellite Score from the US in December 1958, and the landing of a pennant on the Moon by Lunik II (USSR) in September 1959. The first human beings to go into Earth orbit were carried in Vostok I (USSR) in April 1961; and four years later the US launched Early Bird I, the first commercial telecommunications satellite. By 1971 there had been landings on the Moon and Venus, the former manned, and by 1975 space stations with docking facilities were being developed, and Landsat I and II had initiated world surface surveys. The 1980s are witnessing an acceleration of space activities, particularly in telecommunications and broadcasting in the field of Earth surveys and involving space stations, established by both the US and USSR.

Since 1957 close on 14,000 objects have been sent into outer space, of which about 5,000 are still in Earth orbit, most of the remainder have disintegrated in the atmosphere or have been retrieved. The life of Earth satellites depends on their altitude,[1] and an altitude of 200 miles is probably the lowest for a cost-worthy operation.

Given the scale and future expansion of these operations, there has already been much international effort to guide and regulate space activities. The UN system has played an active part and its potential is great. But if we consider some of the general international instruments today, we see that they are no longer adequate or are out of date. Good technical management of space activities calls for the expansion of international agreement on, for example, the allocation and assignment of radio-frequencies, the distribution of geostationary satellite orbits, and the regulation of spillover. Much can be achieved through regional arrangements, exemplified in the ESA Convention (1980) and the Intercosmos Agreement (1977), covering the USSR and Eastern Europe, and there have been many bilateral agreements. But in the principal influences at work there are obstacles to progress and time is running out.

First there is the arms race and the trade in arms. So in a statement on Arms Control Impact the US Senate said in May 1980:

Space systems provide critical strategic and tactical support to military forces and political leaders in the areas of attack, warning, navigation, surveillance, communications, intelligence and meteorology.

The statement expresses the ambivalence of military satellites. They have the capacity to carry weapons of mass destruction and guide them to their targets, and to act as

[1] An altitude of 100 miles will yield a life in orbit of less than two days, but life increases fast for altitudes above 200 miles; for example at 500 miles it will be around 1,000 years. Satellites in geosynchronous orbit are there indefinitely.

anti-satellite weapons. But the surveillance that they can also provide is the first effective means of trans-frontier inspection of the deployment of weapons and forces on or from the ground; and perhaps this surveillance will limit the deployment. But the strategic and tactical support that Earth satellites can offer creates, at least between the major space operators, an imbalance and serves to intensify the arms race, for better defence always demands better attack. So, as a measure of restraint the US–USSR Agreement (1972) limited the establishment of anti-ballistic missile systems to specified areas,[2] but the Agreement appears to have been overtaken by many devices—lasers, particle beams, and killer satellites—and President Reagan spoke in March 1983 of an 'ability to intercept and destroy ballistic missiles before they reached our soil or that of our allies'. Among the anti-satellite devices that are being developed in the US is a missile to be carried in an F15 aircraft and discharged to detonate in a target area of space; and there is being developed in the USSR a manœuvrable satellite carrying conventional explosive for discharge against a target satellite. Yet, if these developments suggest that the capacity of satellite weaponry is being reduced, it must be remembered that lasers can be used to 'blind' satellites, whatever their function—surveillance, defence, or attack.

The capacity of satellites for international surveillance has encouraged both the UN, in December 1982, and the European parliament, in January 1983, to call for the creation of an international surveillance agency. Its task, using Earth satellites, would as envisaged be to monitor the military uses of chemicals and bacteria, the border movements of military forces and nuclear tests or the stockpiling of nuclear material in neutral areas, such as Antarctica. The proposal was characteristically opposed in the UN by both the US and the USSR.

Costing and the choice of programmes are clearly critical factors in all space activities. The impacts of inflation and economic recession, and of insurance demands, can alone present obstacles and limits to space operations. For example, the Chevaline project—the placing of decoys in Polaris

[2] Limited to a single area by Protocol (May 1976).

submarines as 'penetration aids'—was in 1972 to cost
£172m. and by 1983 £1bn. Four accidents, three to satellites
and one to a launcher since 1977, have led to a total of
$192m. being recovered in insurance, and Intelsat has insured
satellites in its latest series for $65–100m.[3] Further, a number
of spacecraft have failed in operation at considerable commercial loss.[4]

The contrasts in the size of space budgets in recent years
have been enormous. The US and USSR budgets are comparable, at least half of the expenditure in each being devoted
to military uses, and far exceed that of any other country or
group of countries. The combined space budgets of the
UK, Federal Republic of Germany, France, and Japan, have
been less than a fifth of either that of the US or USSR. But
it is interesting that space expenditure in the US, as a proportion of total federal outlays, fell from 6 per cent in 1965 to
just over 1 per cent in 1979; and some programmes have
been axed.[5]

An interesting reaction to these budget limitations has
been the negotiations opened between NASA and the ESA
for undertaking joint space probes, four being envisaged:
atmospheric surveys of Mars and Titan,[6] the largest moon of
Saturn; an indicative radar map of Venus; and rendezvous
with comets and asteroids.[7] A possible joint space-station is
also being considered.

Space telecommunications, including broadcasting, also
face competition from the development of cable transmission
and fibre optics, and from schemes such as SHARP (Stationary
high-altitude relay platform), under research in Canada.
Essentially the relay platform would be a vehicle—balloon,

[3] Insurance premiums vary, those for the US space shuttle being about 5 per
cent as compared with 12 per cent paid by ESA for Ariane launches.
[4] Ariane has failed on two launches out of six. USSR failures are seldom
reported but they are known to have occurred.
[5] NASA has cancelled the probe of Halley's Comet in 1986, and the orbiting
of Venus by a radar-equipped satellite; and NOAA (National Oceanic and Atmospheric Administration) plans to end one of its two polar-orbiting weather satellites.
[6] Titan has a dense atmosphere of nitrogen with some methane and possibly
argon, an atmosphere similar to that of the Earth before life emerged.
[7] Asteroids are small bodies, none observed larger than 300 miles in diameter, of which there are about 1,500 in a belt around the Sun between Mars
and Jupiter.

helicopter, or ultra-light aircraft—powered from the ground and moving in a small circle at an altitude of about twelve miles. Its relay broadcast signals would have a range of about 500 km and it would be far cheaper and also longer-lived than a satellite.[8]

The role of private enterprise in space activities is increasing and is becoming, as in other areas, ambiguous as well as competitive. In the first place space operations are markedly mixed, in that industrial enterprises, governmental agencies, and international organizations all participate in them; indeed given the scale of their operations, and the volume of public finance that may contribute to them, it is hard to describe the major industrial enterprises as private, even though they are independent companies in law.

The industrial enterprises work through sub-contracting joint ventures, and investment, and the establishment of consortia, and may co-operate with governmental agencies. To recall some evidence of this, an example of a consortium in United Satellites, constituted by British Aerospace, British Telecom, and GEC Marconi, to build three communication satellites for launch in 1986 with two TV channels. The European Space Agency has chosen six enterprises to assist in the planning of manned stations in space; British Aerospace, Matra (France), one Italian company, and three companies in the Federal Republic of Germany. Aerospatiale and Thomson CSF, of France, and two German companies have formed a consortium for the construction of a direct TV broadcasting satellite; and more Ariane launchers are being built by Arianespace, a French enterprise, of which CNES, Aerospatiale, and Matra hold the majority of shares.

Further, a number of aerospace companies in Europe have formed a common policy group, named Eurospace, concerned with possible programmes and the role of the European Space Agency.

These examples of industrial and commercial practice illustrate the fact that the construction of spacecraft and launchers, launching operations, and the control and functioning of satellites in orbit, are combined operations, both

[8] *New Scientist* (26.5.1983).

nationally and internationally. Only perhaps in the United
States and the USSR can these combined operations be all
carried out in one country: for example, in 1980 the United
Kingdom devoted three-quarters of its £80m. space budget
to European Space Agency projects.

Nevertheless, even with the establishment of Intelsat as
a form of public corporation, the field is still open to competition from private enterprise. Intelsat's scale of operations
—seventeen communications satellites—and demonstrable
profits, make its field attractive. Its economic position is
protected by the provision in the founding convention that
its common carrier traffic shall not be competed with. But
how much of its traffic can be so described? At least one
US enterprise is seeking licence from the Federal Communications Commission to operate privately owned transatlantic
satellites.

But private enterprise can be restricted, as often, by
necessary public regulations. So US companies require a
licence from NASA to launch satellites; and, on a larger scale,
the ITU, through its World Administrative Conference, fixes
the spacing of geostationary satellites, normally separated
by four degrees or around 3,000 km in order to prevent
mutual interference. Twelve US companies are seeking to
put as many as fifty satellites into orbit for beaming TV
programmes to roof-top aerials. These plans are contested
by a number of countries in the Americas, which fear an
overcrowding of geostationary orbits. It will be for the
WARC to decide.

This recognition of the need to conserve natural resources
is also reflected in more general concern about the state of
the environment. The full environmental effects of space
operations remain to be seen, for the impact of rocket
exhausts is not negligible. But in remote sensing by satellites,
there is also a positive contribution, not only to the economic needs of countries, and particularly the less developed,
but also the conservation of natural resources and the preservation of the environment; so there, as always, a balancing
of policies is needed.[9]

[9] In a report of the US National Academy of Sciences in 1966 it was said:
'Rocket-exhaust contamination of the higher atmosphere is however, a much

Since satellite transmissions can cover the globe, access to them is as physically possible for the *Third World* as any other part. But access depends not only upon the establishment of a satellite in orbit within reach of a country, but, more important, the ability of the country to finance the ground stations needed to receive and distribute satellite transmissions. The prospect is at present dim. Take Africa. Only one ground-station, in Johannesburg, receives directly Landsat transmissions, and the rest of the continent depends for the needed information on data sent in computer tapes from the US or Europe. Negotiations have been undertaken with both the European Community and IBRD (International Bank for Reconstruction and Development) to finance three ground-stations—in Kenya, Upper Volta, and Zaïre—at a cost of $15-20 million each. Further, a review of new space operations planned for 1983-90 shows none serving the special interests of developing countries. India stands out as a country embarked on a satellite programme. It launched two satellites in 1981, one short-lived, and Ford Aerospace in the US is building two multi-purpose geostationary satellites for it. India is spending on space operations almost as much as the UK.

But few developing countries have yet sufficient receivers for the reception of satellite TV broadcasting, for example, of educational programmes; and many have difficult terrain and scattered populations, which in any case make programme distribution difficult over land. The reception of satellite broadcast programmes should then be a target of aid to developing countries.

To conclude—the complexity of space operations, and the difficulties of regulating them at so many different levels, are manifest, and perhaps no human activity has ever been so basically international. Much has still to be done, in the common interests of all countries and their peoples,

more complex problem, primarily because the chemistry of the mesosphere and thermosphere (including the radiational roles played by the minor constituents) and the processes in those regions that disperse or remove impurities are so little understood. Since rocket activity will increase, and since we are already capable of doubling in a single year, the quantity of some exotic constituents (e.g. atomic sodium), vigorous investigation of aeronomy and high-atmosphere dynamics is a clear pre-requisite to settling the issue of rocket-caused contamination.'

to secure effective outer space practices across all frontiers, not least proper control of military uses of outer space. Much has still to be done in gaining access to and use of information obtained in satellites and in protecting the upper atmosphere from pollution, and natural resources from maldistribution and waste.

The opportunities and dangers of space operations are together without precedent in history.

Principal Events

Space Operations

1957	4 October. Sputnik 1 launched (USSR).
1958	18 December. US launched first telecommunications satellite.
1959	9 September. Lunik 2 (USSR) landed pennant on the Moon.
1961	12 February. Venus 1 (USSR) landed on Venus.
	4 April. Vostok 1 (USSR) launched first human beings into Earth orbit.
1962	7 March. OSO 1 (US) launched: first satellite observatory.
1965	6 April. Early Bird (US) launched: first commercial communications satellite.
1969	July. Apollo 11 (US) landed on the Moon and crew brought back rock and dust samples.
1973	July. Skylab 2 (US) rendezvous with orbiting laboratory (59 days in space).
1975	July. Apollo (US) and Soyuz (USSR) test docking.
1978	24 January. Cosmos 954 fell in Canada.
1981	19 June. Cosmos 1267 joined Salyut 6 (USSR).
1983	June. Challenger (US) joined space station.

International action

1960	US agreements on tracking of satellites with Canada, Ecuador, Mexico, Nigeria, South Africa, Spain, United Kingdom.
	Unesco Resolution 12/5. 1322 on educational uses of satellites.
1963	US, UK, USSR Agreement banning nuclear weapon tests in outer space.
	UN General Assembly Resolutions 1962 and 1963–XVIII on space.

1967   10 October. Outer Space Treaty in force.
1972   July. Intersputnik Agreement in force.
        1 September. Convention on Liability for Damage
        from Space Operations in force.
1973   12 February. Intelsat Definitive Arrangements in
        force.
1975   May. ESA Agreement concluded.
1977   25 March. Intercosmos Agreement in force: text in
        International Legal Materials XVI (1977), 1.
1979   Inmarsat Convention in force: text in *International
        Legal Materials* XV (1976), 105, 219.
        Draft Moon Agreement adopted.
1980   30 October. ESA Agreement in force.

APPENDIX B

Documents

Outer Space Treaty (1967)

Preamble

The States parties to this treaty,

Inspired by the great prospects opening up before mankind as a result of man's entry into outer space;

Recognizing the common interest of all mankind in the progress of the exploration and use of outer space for peaceful purposes;

Believing that the exploration and use of outer space should be carried on for the benefit of all peoples irrespective of the degree of their economic or scientific development;

Desiring to contribute to broad international co-operation in the scientific as well as the legal aspects of the exploration and use of outer space for peaceful purposes;

Believing that such co-operation will contribute to the development of mutual understanding and to the strengthening of friendly relations between States and peoples;

Recalling [the] Resolution entitled 'Declaration of Legal Principles Governing the Activities of States in the Exploration and Use of Outer Space,' which was adopted unanimously by the U.N. General Assembly on 13 December 1963;

Recalling [the] Resolution calling upon States to refrain from placing in orbit around the earth any objects carrying nuclear weapons or any other kinds of weapons of mass destruction or from installing such weapons on celestial bodies, which was adopted unanimously by the U.N. General Assembly on 17 October 1963.

Taking account of [the] U.N. General Assembly Resolution of 3 November 1947, which condemned propaganda designed or likely to provoke or encourage any threat to the peace, breach of the peace, or act of aggression and considering that the aforementioned resolution is applicable to outer space;

Convinced that a treaty on principles governing the activities of States in the exploration and use of outer space, including the moon and other celestial bodies, will further the purposes and principles of the Charter of the United Nations;

Have agreed on the following:

Article 1

The exploration and use of outer space, including the moon and other celestial bodies, shall be carried out for the benefit and in the interests of all countries, irrespective of their degree of economic or scientific development, and shall be the province of all mankind.

Outer space including the moon and other celestial bodies, shall be free for exploration and use by all States without discrimination of any kind, on a basis of equality and in accordance with international law, and there shall be free access to all areas of celestial bodies.

There shall be freedom of scientific investigation in outer space, including the moon and other celestial bodies, and States shall facilitate and encourage international co-operation in such investigation.

Article 2

Outer space, including the moon and other celestial bodies, is not subject to national appropriation by claim of sovereignty, by means of use of occupation, or by any other means.

Article 3

States parties to the treaty shall carry on activities in the exploration and use of outer space, including the moon and other celestial bodies, in accordance with international law, including the Charter of the United Nations, in the interest of maintaining international peace and security and promoting international co-operation and understanding.

Article 4

States parties to the treaty undertake not to place in orbit around the earth any objects carrying nuclear weapons or any other kinds of weapons of mass destruction, install such weapons on celestial bodies, or station such weapons in outer space in any other manner.

The moon and other celestial bodies shall be used by all States parties to the treaty exclusively for peaceful purposes. The establishment of military bases, installations, and fortifications, the testing of any type of weapons, and the conduct of military manœuvres on celestial bodies shall be forbidden. The use of military personnel for scientific research or for any other peaceful purposes shall not be prohibited. The use of any equipment or facility necessary for peaceful exploration of the moon and other celestial bodies shall also not be prohibited.

Article 5

States parties to the treaty shall regard astronauts as envoys of mankind in outer space and shall render to them all possible assistance in the event of accident, distress, or emergency landing on the territory of another State party or on the high seas. When astronauts make such a landing, they shall be safely and promptly returned to the State of registry of their space vehicle.

In carrying on activities in outer space and on celestial bodies, the astronauts of one State party shall render all possible assistance to the astronauts of other States parties.

States parties to the treaty shall immediately inform the other States parties to the treaty or the Secretary-General of the United Nations of any phenomena they discover in outer space, including the moon and other celestial bodies, which could constitute a danger to the life or health of astronauts.

Article 6

States parties to the treaty shall bear international responsibility for national activities in outer space, including the moon and other celestial bodies, whether such activities are carried on by governmental agencies or by non-governmental entities, and for assuring that national activities are carried out in conformity with the provisions set forth in the present treaty.

The activities of non-governmental entities in outer space,

including the moon and other celestial bodies, shall require authorization and continuing supervision by the State concerned. When activities are carried on in outer space, including the moon and other celestial bodies, by an international organization, responsibility for compliance with this treaty shall be borne both by the international organization and by the States parties to the treaty participating in such organization.

Article 7

Each State party to the treaty that launches or procures the launching of an object into outer space, including the moon and other celestial bodies, and each State party from whose territory or facility an object is launched, is internationally liable for damage to another State party to the treaty or to its natural or juridical persons by such object or its component parts on the earth, in airspace, or in outer space, including the moon and other celestial bodies.

Article 8

A State party to the treaty on whose registry an object launched into outer space is carried shall retain jurisdiction and control over such object, and over any personnel thereof, while in outer space or on a celestial body. Ownership of objects launched into outer space, including objects landed or constructed on a celestial body, and of their component parts, is not affected by their presence in outer space, including the body, or by their return to the earth. Such objects or component parts found beyond the limits of the State party to the treaty on whose registry they are carried shall be returned to that State, which shall, upon request, furnish identifying data prior to their return.

Article 9

In the exploration and use of outer space, including the moon and other celestial bodies, States parties to the treaty shall be guided by the principle of co-operation and mutual assistance and shall conduct all their activities in outer space, including the moon and other celestial bodies, with due regard to the corresponding interests of all States parties to the treaty.

States parties to the treaty shall pursue studies of outer space, including the moon and other celestial bodies, and conduct exploration of them so as to avoid their harmful contamination and also adverse changes in the environment of the Earth resulting from the introduction of extraterrestrial matter, and, where necessary, shall adopt appropriate measures for this purpose.

If a State party to the treaty has reason to believe that an activity or experiment planned by it or its nationals in outer space, including the moon and other celestial bodies, would cause potentially harmful interference with activities of other States parties in the peaceful exploration and use of outer space, including the moon and other celestial bodies, it shall undertake appropriate international consultations before proceeding with any such activity or experiment.

A State party to the treaty which has reason to believe that an activity or experiment planned by another State party in outer space, including the moon and other celestial bodies, would cause potentially harmful interference with activities in the peaceful exploration and use of outer space, including the moon and other celestial bodies, may request consultation concerning the activity or experiment.

Article 10

In order to promote international co-operation in the exploration and use of outer space, including the moon and other celestial bodies, in conformity with the purposes of this treaty, the States parties to the treaty shall consider on a basis of equality any requests by other States parties to the treaty to be afforded an opportunity to observe the flight of space objects launched by those States. The nature of such an opportunity for observation and the conditions under which it could be afforded shall be determined by agreement between the States concerned.

Article 11

In order to promote international co-operation in the peaceful exploration and use of outer space, States parties to the treaty conducting activities in outer space, including the moon and other celestial bodies, agree to inform the

Secretary-General of the United Nations as well as the public
and the international scientific community, to the greatest
extent feasible and practicable, of the nature, conduct,
locations, and results of such activities. On receiving the said
information, the U.N. Secretary-General should be prepared
to disseminate it immediately and effectively.

Article 12

All stations, installations, equipment, and space vehicles on
the moon and other celestial bodies shall be open to representatives of other States parties to the treaty, on a basis of
reciprocity. Such representatives shall give reasonable advance
notice of a projected visit, in order that appropriate consultations may be held and that maximum precautions may be
taken to assure safety and to avoid interference with normal
operations in the facility to be visited.

Article 13

The provisions of this treaty shall apply to the activities of
States parties to the treaty in the exploration and use of
outer space, including the moon and other celestial bodies,
whether such activities are carried on by a single State party
to the treaty or jointly with other States, including cases
where they are carried on within the framework of international inter-governmental organizations.

Any practical questions arising in connexion with activities
carried on by international inter-governmental organizations
in the exploration and use of outer space, including the moon
and other celestial bodies, shall be resolved by the States
parties to the treaty either with the appropriate international
organization or with one or more State members of that
international organization, which are parties to this treaty.

Article 14

(1) This treaty shall be open to all States for signature.
Any State which does not sign this treaty before its entry
into force in accordance with Paragraph 3 of this Article may
accede to it any time.

(2) This treaty shall be subject to ratification by signatory
States. Instruments of ratification and of accession shall be

deposited with the Governments of the Union of Soviet Socialist Republics, the United Kingdom of Great Britain and Northern Ireland, and the United States of America, which are hereby designated the Depositary Governments.

(3) This treaty shall enter into force upon the deposit of instruments of ratification by five Governments, including the Governments designated as Depositary Governments.

(4) For States whose instruments of ratification or accession are deposited subsequent to the entry into force of this treaty, it shall enter into force on the date of the deposit of their instruments of ratification or accession.

(5) The Depositary Governments shall promptly inform all signatory and acceding States of the date of each signature, the date of deposit of each instrument of ratification of and accession to this treaty, the date of its entry into force, and other notices.

(6) This treaty shall be registered by the Depositary Governments pursuant to Article 102 of the U.N. Charter.

Article 15

Any State party to the treaty may propose amendments to this treaty. Amendments shall enter into force for each State party to the treaty accepting the amendments upon their acceptance by a majority of the States parties to the treaty, and thereafter for each remaining State party to the treaty on the date of acceptance by it.

Article 16

Any State party to the treaty may give notice of its withdrawal from the treaty one year after its entry into force by written notification to the Depositary Governments. Such withdrawal shall take effect one year from the date of receipt of this notification.

Article 17

This treaty of which the Chinese, English, French, Russian, and Spanish texts are equally authentic, shall be deposited in the archives of the Depositary Governments.

Agreement on Activities of States on the Moon and other Celestial Bodies (UN General Assembly Resolution 34/68)

'The states parties to this Agreement,

'Noting the achievements of states in the exploration and use of the moon and other celestial bodies,

'Recognizing that the moon, as a natural satellite of the earth, has an important role to play in the exploration of outer space,

'Determined to promote on the basis of equality the further development of co-operation among states in the exploration and use of the moon and other celestial bodies,

'Desiring to prevent the moon from becoming an area of international conflict,

'Bearing in mind the benefits which may be derived from the exploitation of the natural resources of the moon and other celestial bodies,

'Recalling the Treaty on Principles governing the Activities of States in the Exploration and Use of Outer Space, including the Moon and Other Celestial Bodies [of 1966—see 21791 A; 22360 A], the Agreement on the Rescue of Astronauts, the Return of Astronauts and the Return of Objects launched into Outer Space [of 1967—see 22539 A; 23192 A], the Convention on International Liability for Damage caused by Space Objects [of 1971—see 25192 A], and the Convention on Registration of Objects launched into Outer Space [of 1974—see page 26949],

'Taking into account the need to define and develop the provisions of these international instruments in relation to the moon and other celestial bodies, having regard to further progress in the exploration and use of outer space,

'Have agreed on the following:

Article 1

'(1) The provisions of this Agreement relating to the moon shall also apply to other celestial bodies within the solar system, other than the earth, except in so far as specific legal norms enter into force with respect to any of these celestial bodies.

'(2) For the purposes of this Agreement reference to the

Moon shall include orbits around or other trajectories to or around it.

'(3) This Agreement does not apply to extraterrestrial materials which reach the surface of the earth by natural means.

Article 2

'All activities on the moon, including its exploration and use, shall be carried out in accordance with international law, in particular the Charter of the United Nations, and taking into account the Declaration of Principles of International Law concerning Friendly Relations and Co-operation among States in accordance with the Charter of the United Nations, adopted by the General Assembly on Oct. 24, 1970, in the interests of maintaining international peace and security and promoting international co-operation and mutual understanding, and with due regard to the corresponding interests of all other states parties. [For the 1970 Declaration on Principles of International Law, see page 24418.]

Article 3

'(1) The moon shall be used by all states parties exclusively for peaceful purposes.

'(2) Any threat or use of force or any other hostile act or threat of hostile act on the moon is prohibited. It is likewise prohibited to use the moon in order to commit any such act or to engage in any such threat in relation to the earth, the moon, spacecraft, the personnel of spacecraft or man-made space objects.

'(3) States parties shall not place in orbit around or other trajectory to or around the moon objects carrying nuclear weapons or any other kinds of weapons of mass destruction or place or use such weapons on or in the moon.

'(4) The establishment of military bases, installations and fortifications, the testing of any type of weapons and the conduct of military manœuvres on the moon shall be forbidden. The use of military personnel for scientific research or for any other peaceful purposes shall not be prohibited. The use of any equipment or facility necessary for peaceful exploration and use of the moon shall also not be prohibited.

Article 4

'(1) The exploration and use of the moon shall be the province of all mankind and shall be carried out for the benefit and in the interests of all countries, irrespective of their degree of economic or scientific development. Due regard shall be paid to the interests of present and future generations as well as to the need to promote higher standards of living and conditions of economic and social progress and development in accordance with the Charter of the United Nations.

'(2) States parties shall be guided by the principle of co-operation and mutual assistance in all their activities concerning the exploration and use of the moon. International co-operation in pursuance of this Agreement should be as wide as possible and may take place on a multilateral basis, on a bilateral basis or through international inter-governmental organizations.

Article 5

'(1) States parties shall inform the Secretary-General of the United Nations as well as the public and the international scientific community, to the greatest extent feasible and practicable, of their activities concerned with the exploration and use of the moon. Information on the time, purposes, locations, orbital parameters and duration shall be given in respect of each mission to the moon as soon as possible after launching, while information on the results of each mission, including scientific results, shall be furnished upon completion of the mission. In the case of a mission lasting more than 60 days, information on conduct of the mission, including any scientific results, shall be given periodically at 30-day intervals. For missions lasting more than six months, only significant additions to such information need be reported thereafter.

'(2) If a state party becomes aware that another state party plans to operate simultaneously in the same area of or in the same orbit around or trajectory to or around the moon, it shall promptly inform the other state of the timing of and plans for its own operations.

'(3) In carrying out activities under this Agreement, states parties shall promptly inform the Secretary-General, as well as the public and the international scientific community, of any phenomena they discover in outer space, including the moon, which could endanger human life or health, as well as of any indication of organic life.

Article 6

'(1) There shall be freedom of scientific investigation on the moon by all states parties without discrimination of any kind, on the basis of equality and in accordance with international law.

'(2) In carrying out scientific investigations and in furtherance of the provisions of this Agreement, the states parties shall have the right to collect on and remove from the moon samples of its mineral and other substances. Such samples shall remain at the disposal of those states parties which caused them to be collected and may be used by them for scientific purposes. States parties shall have regard to the desirability of making a portion of such samples available to other interested state parties and the international scientific community for scientific investigation. States parties may in the course of scientific investigations also use mineral and other substances of the moon in quantities appropriate for the support of their missions.

'(3) States parties agree on the desirability of exchanging scientific and other personnel on expeditions to or installations on the moon to the greatest extent feasible and practicable.

Article 7

'(1) In exploring and using the moon, states parties shall take measures to prevent the disruption of the existing balance of its environment whether by introducing adverse changes in that environment, by its harmful contamination through the introduction of extra-environmental matter or otherwise. States parties shall also take measures to avoid harmfully affecting the environment of the earth through the introduction of extraterrestrial matter or otherwise.

'(2) States parties shall inform the Secretary-General of the

United Nations of the measures being adopted by them in accordance with Paragraph 1 of this Article and shall also, to the maximum extent feasible, notify him in advance of all placements by them of radio-active materials on the moon and of the purposes of such placements.

'(3) States parties shall report to other states parties and to the Secretary-General concerning areas of the moon having special scientific interest in order that, without prejudice to the rights of other states parties, consideration may be given to the designation of such areas as international scientific preserves for which special protective arrangements are to be agreed upon in consultation with the competent bodies of the United Nations.

Article 8

'(1) States parties may pursue their activities in the exploration and use of the moon anywhere on or below its surface, subject to the provisions of this Agreement.

'(2) For these purposes states parties may, in particular:

'(*a*) Land their space objects on the moon and launch them from the moon;

'(*b*) Place their personnel, space vehicles, equipment, facilities, stations and installations anywhere on or below the surface of the moon.

'Personnel, space vehicles, equipment, facilities, stations and installations may move or be moved freely over or below the surface of the moon.

'(3) Activities of states parties in accordance with Paragraphs 1 and 2 of this Article shall not interfere with the activities of other states parties on the moon. Where such interference may occur, the states parties concerned shall undertake consultations in accordance with Article 15, Paragraphs 2 and 3 of this Agreement.

Article 9

'(1) States parties may establish manned and unmanned stations on the moon. A state party establishing a station shall use only that area which is required for the needs of the station and shall immediately inform the Secretary-General of the United Nations of the location and purposes of that station. Subsequently, at annual intervals that state shall like-wise inform the Secretary-General whether the station continues in use and whether its purposes have changed.

'(2) Stations shall be installed in such a manner that they do not impede the free access to all areas of the moon by personnel, vehicles and equipment of other states parties conducting activities on the moon in accordance with the provisions of this Agreement or of Article 1 of the Treaty on Principles governing the Activities of States in the Exploration and Use of Outer Space, including the Moon and Other Celestial Bodies.

Article 10

'(1) States parties shall adopt all practicable measures to safeguard the life and health of persons on the moon. For this purpose they shall regard any person on the moon as an astronaut within the meaning of Article V of the Treaty on Principles governing the Activities of States in the Exploration and Use of Outer Space, including the Moon and Other Celestial Bodies and as part of the personnel of a spacecraft within the meaning of the Agreement of the Rescue of Astronauts, the Return of Astronauts and the Return of Objects launched into Outer Space.

'(2) States parties shall offer shelter in their stations, installations, vehicles and other facilities to persons in distress on the moon.

Article 11

'(1) The moon and its natural resources are the common heritage of mankind, which finds its expression in the provisions of this Agreement, in particular in Paragraph 5 of this Article.

'(2) The moon is not subject to national appropriation by any claim of sovereignty, by means of use or occupation, or by any other means.

'(3) Neither the surface nor the subsurface of the moon, nor any part thereof or natural resources in place, shall become property of any state, international intergovernmental or non-governmental organization, national organization or non-governmental entity or of any natural person. The placement of personnel, space vehicles, equipment, facilities, stations and installations on or below the surface of the moon, including structures connected with its surface or subsurface, shall not create a right of ownership over the surface or the subsurface of the moon or any areas thereof. The foregoing provisions are without prejudice to the international regime referred to in Paragraph 5 of this Article.

'(4) States parties have the right to exploration and use of the moon without discrimination of any kind, on the basis of equality and in accordance with international law and the provisions of this Agreement.

'(5) States parties to this Agreement hereby undertake to establish an international regime, including appropriate procedures, to govern the exploitation of the natural resources of the moon as such exploitation is about to become feasible. This provision shall be implemented in accordance with Article 18 of this Agreement.

'(6) In order to facilitate the establishment of the international regime referred to in Paragraph 5 of this Article, states parties shall inform the Secretary-General of the United Nations as well as the public and the international scientific community, to the greatest extent feasible and practicable, of any natural resources they may discover on the moon.

'(7) The main purposes of the international regime to be established shall include:

'(*a*) The orderly and safe development of the natural resources of the moon;

'(*b*) The rational management of those resources;

'(*c*) The expansion of opportunities in the use of those resources;

'(*d*) An equitable sharing by all states parties in the benefits derived from those resources, whereby the interests and needs of the developing countries, as well as the efforts of those countries, which have contributed either directly or indirectly to the exploration of the moon, shall be given special consideration.

'(8) All the activities with respect to the natural resources of the moon shall be carried out in a manner compatible with the purposes specified in Paragraph 7 of this Article

Documents 139

and the provisions of Article 6, Paragraph 2, of this Agreement.

Article 12

'(1) States parties shall retain jurisdiction and control over their personnel, space vehicles, equipment, facilities, stations and installations on the moon. The ownership of space vehicles, equipment, facilities, stations and installations shall not be affected by their presence on the moon.

'(2) Vehicles, installations and equipment or their component parts found in places other than their intended location shall be dealt with in accordance with Article 5 of the Agreement on the Rescue of Astronauts, the Return of Astronauts and the Return of Objects, launched into Outer Space.

'(3) In the event of an emergency involving a threat to human life, states parties may use the equipment, vehicles, installations, facilities, or supplies of other states parties on the moon. Prompt notification of such use shall be made to the Secretary-General of the United Nations or the state party concerned.

Article 13

'A State party which learns of the crash-landing, forced landing or other unintended landing on the moon of a space object, or its component parts, that were not launched by it, shall promptly inform the launching state party and the Secretary-General of the United Nations.

Article 14

'(1) States parties to this Agreement shall bear international responsibility for national activities on the moon, whether such activities are carried out by governmental agencies or by non-governmental entities, and for assuring that national activities are carried out in conformity with the provisions set forth in this Agreement. States parties shall ensure that non-governmental entities under their jurisdiction shall engage in activities on the moon only under the authority and continuing supervision of the appropriate state party.

'(2) States parties recognize that detailed arrangements

concerning liability for damage caused on the moon, in addition to the provisions of the Treaty on Principles governing the Activities of States in the Exploration and Use of Outer Space, including the Moon and Other Celestial Bodies and the Convention on International Liability for Damage caused by Space Objects, may become necessary as a result of more extensive activities on the moon. Any such arrangements shall be elaborated in accordance with the procedure provided for in Article 18 of this Agreement.

Article 15

'(1) Each state party may assure itself that the activities of other states parties in the exploration and use of the moon are compatible with the provisions of this Agreement. To this end, all space vehicles, equipment, facilities, stations and installations on the moon shall be open to other state parties. Such states parties shall give reasonable advance notice of a projected visit, in order that appropriate consultations may be held and that maximum precautions may be taken to assure safety and to avoid interference with normal operations in the facility to be visited. In pursuance of this Article, any state party may act on its own behalf or with the full or partial assistance of any other state party or through appropriate international procedures within the framework of the United Nations and in accordance with the Charter.

'(2) A state party which has reason to believe that another state party is not fulfilling the obligations incumbent upon it pursuant to this Agreement or that another state party is interfering with the rights which the former state has under this Agreement may request consultations with that state party. A state party receiving such a request shall enter into such consultations without delay. Any other state party which requests to do so shall be entitled to take part in the consultations. Each state party participating in such consultations shall seek a mutually acceptable resolution of any controversy and shall bear in mind the rights and interests of all states parties. The Secretary-General of the United Nations shall be informed of the results of the consultations and shall transmit the information received to all states parties concerned.

'(3) If the consultations do not lead to a mutually acceptable settlement which has due regard for the rights and
interests of all states parties, the parties concerned shall take
all measures to settle the dispute by other peaceful means
of their choice appropriate to the circumstances and the
nature of the dispute. If difficulties arise in connexion with
the opening of consultations, or if consultations do not lead
to a mutually acceptable settlement, any state party may
seek the assistance of the Secretary-General, without seeking
the consent of any other state party concerned, in order to
resolve the controversy. A state party which does not maintain diplomatic relations with another state party concerned
shall participate in such consultations, as its choice, either
itself or through another state party or the Secretary-General
as intermediary.

Article 16

'With the exception of Articles 17 to 21, references in this
Agreement to states shall be deemed to apply to any international inter-governmental organization which conducts
space activities if the organization declares its acceptance of
the rights and obligations provided for in this Agreement and
if a majority of the states members of the organization are
states parties to this Agreement and to the Treaty of Principles governing the Activities of States in the Exploration
and Use of Outer Space, including the Moon and Other
Celestial Bodies, states members of any such organization
which are states parties to this Agreement shall take all
appropriate steps to ensure that the organization makes a
declaration in accordance with the provisions of this Article.

Article 17

'Any state party to this Agreement may propose amendments to the Agreement. Amendments shall enter into force
for each state party to the Agreement accepting the amendments upon their acceptance by a majority of the states
parties to the Agreement and thereafter for each remaining
state party to the Agreement on the date of acceptance by it.

.*Article 18*

'Ten years after the entry into force of this Agreement, the question of the review of the Agreement shall be included in the provisional agenda of the General Assembly of the United Nations in order to consider, in the light of past application of the Agreement, whether it requires revision. However, at any time after the Agreement has been in force for five years, the Secretary-General of the United Nations, as depository, shall, at the request of one-third of the states parties to the Agreement and with the concurrence of the majority of the states parties, convene a conference of the states parties to review this agreement. A review conference shall also consider the question of the implementation of the provisions of Article 11, Paragraph 5, on the basis of the principle referred to in Paragraph 1 of that Article and taking into account in particular any relevant technological developments.

Article 19

'(1) This Agreement shall be open for signature by all states at United Nations Headquarters in New York.

'(2) This Agreement shall be subject to ratification by signatory states. Any state which does not sign this Agreement before its entry into force in accordance with Paragraph 3 of this Article may accede to it at any time. Instruments of ratification or accession shall be deposited with the Secretary-General of the United Nations.

'(3) This Agreement shall enter into force on the 30th day following the date of deposit of the fifth instrument of ratification.

'(4) For each state depositing its instrument of ratification or accession after the entry into force of this Agreement, it shall enter into force on the 30th day following the date of deposit of any such instrument.

'(5) The Secretary-General shall promptly inform all signatory and acceding states of the date of each signature, the date of deposit of each instrument of ratification or accession to this Agreement, the date of its entry into force and other notices.

Article 20

'Any state party to this Agreement may give notice of its withdrawal from the Agreement one year after its entry into force by written notification to the Secretary-General of the United Nations. Such withdrawal shall take effect one year from the date of receipt of this notification.

Article 21

'The original of this Agreement, of which the Arabic, Chinese, English, French, Russian and Spanish texts are equally authentic, shall be deposited with the Secretary-General of the United Nations, who shall send certified copies thereof to all signatory and acceding states.'

The Agreement was opened for signature in New York on Dec. 18, 1979, and as stated in Article 19 would require ratification by five signatories to enter into force—(UN Office of Public Information, New York) (*Prev. rep. page 30225; Lunar Research pages 28986, 28030-31, 25685 A; Outer Space Treaties, Agreements and Conventions 21791 A, 22539 A, 25192 A, page 26949*)

Convention on International Liability for Damage caused by Space Objects (1972)

The States Parties to this Convention

Recognizing the common interest of all mankind in furthering the exploration and use of outer space for peaceful purposes,

Recalling the Treaty on Principles Governing the Activities of States in the Exploration and Use of Outer Space, including the Moon and Other Celestial Bodies,

Taking into consideration that, notwithstanding the precautionary measures to be taken by States and international intergovernmental organizations involved in the launching of space objects, damage may on occasion be caused by such objects,

Recognizing the need to elaborate effective international rules and procedures concerning liability for damage caused by space objects and to ensure, in particular, the prompt payment under the terms of this Convention of a full and equitable measure of compensation to victims of such damage,

Believing that the establishment of such rules and procedures will contribute to the strengthening of international co-operation in the field of the exploration and use of outer space for peaceful purposes,

Have agreed on the following:

Article I

For the purposes of this Convention:

(a) the term 'damage' means loss of life, personal injury or other impairment of health; or loss of or damage to property of States or of persons, natural or juridical, or property of international intergovernmental organizations;

(b) the term 'launching' includes attempted launching;

(c) the term 'launching State' means:

(1) a State which launches or procures the launching of a space object;

(2) a State from whose territory or facility a space object is launched;

(d) the term 'space object' includes component parts of a space object as well as its launch vehicle and parts thereof.

Article II

A launching State shall be absolutely liable to pay compensation for damage caused by its space object on the surface of the earth or to aircraft in flight.

Article III

In the event of damage being caused elsewhere than on the surface of the earth to a space object of one launching State or to persons or property on board such a space object by a space object of another launching State, the latter shall be liable only if the damage is due to its fault or the fault of the persons for whom it is responsible.

Article IV

1. In the event of damage being caused elsewhere than on the surface of the earth to a space object of one launching State or to persons or property on board such a space object of another launching State, and of damage thereby being caused to a third State or to its natural or juridical persons, the first two States shall be jointly and severally liable to the third State, to the extent indicated by the following:

(*a*) if the damage has been caused to the third State on the surface of the earth or to aircraft in flight, their liability to the third State shall be absolute;

(*b*) if the damage has been caused to a space object of the third State or to persons or property on board that space object elsewhere than on the surface of the earth, their liability to the third State shall be based on the fault of either of the first two States or on the fault of persons for whom either is responsible.

2. In all cases of joint and several liability referred to in paragraph 1, the burden of compensation for the damage shall be apportioned between the first two States in accordance with the extent to which they were at fault; if the extent of the fault of each of these States cannot be established, the burden of compensation shall be apportioned equally between them. Such apportionment shall be without prejudice to the right of the third State to seek the entire compensation due under this Convention from any or all

of the launching States which are jointly and severally liable.

Article V

1. Whenever two or more States jointly launch a space object, they shall be jointly and severally liable for any damage caused.

2. A launching State which has paid compensation for damage shall have the right to present a claim for indemnification to other participants in the joint launching. The participants in a joint launching may conclude agreements regarding the apportioning among themselves of the financial obligation in respect of which they are jointly and severally liable. Such agreements shall be without prejudice to the right of a State sustaining damage to seek the entire compensation due under this Convention from any or all of the launching States which are jointly and severally liable.

3. A State from whose territory or facility a space object is launched shall be regarded as a participant in a joint launching.

Article VI

1. Subject to the provisions of paragraph 2, exoneration from absolute liability shall be granted to the extent that a launching State establishes that the damage has resulted either wholly or partially from gross negligence or from an act or omission done with intent to cause damage on the part of a claimant State or of natural or juridical persons it represents.

2. No exoneration whatever shall be granted in cases where the damage has resulted from activities conducted by a launching State which are not in conformity with international law including, in particular, the Charter of the United Nations and the Treaty on Principles Governing the Activities of States in the Exploration and Use of Outer Space, including the Moon and Other Celestial Bodies.

Article VII

The provisions of this Convention shall not apply to damage caused by a space object of a launching State to:

(*a*) nationals of that launching State;

(*b*) foreign nationals during such time as they are participating or at any stage thereafter until its descent, or during such time as they are in the immediate vicinity of a planned launching or recovery area as the result of an invitation by that launching State.

Article VIII

1. A State which suffers damage, or whose natural or juridical persons suffer damage, may present to a launching State a claim for compensation for such damage.

2. If the State of nationality has not presented a claim, another State may, in respect of damage sustained in its territory by any natural or juridical person, present a claim to a launching State.

3. If neither the State of nationality nor the State in whose territory the damage was sustained has presented a claim or notified its intention of presenting a claim, another State may, in respect of damage sustained by its permanent residents, present a claim to a launching State.

Article IX

A claim for compensation for damage shall be presented to a launching State through diplomatic channels. If a State does not maintain diplomatic relations with the launching State concerned, it may request another State to present its interests under this Convention. It may also present its interests under this Convention. It may also present its claim through the Secretary-General of the United Nations, provided the claimant State and the launching State are both Members of the United Nations.

1. A claim for compensation for damage may be presented to a launching State not later than one year following the date of the occurrence of the damage or the identification of the launching State which is liable.

2. If, however, a State does not know of the occurrence of the damage or has not been able to identify the launching State which is liable, it may present a claim within one year following the date on which it learned of the aforementioned facts; however, this period shall in no event exceed one year

following the date on which the State could reasonably be expected to have learned of the facts through the exercise of due diligence.

3. The time-limits specified in paragraphs 1 and 2 shall apply even if the full extent of the damage may not be known. In this event, however, the claimant State shall be entitled to revise the claim and submit additional documentation after the expiration of such time-limits until one year after the full extent of the damage is known.

Article XI

1. Presentation of a claim to a launching State for compensation for damage under this Convention shall not require the prior exhaustion of any local remedies which may be available to a claimant State or to natural or juridical persons it represents.

2. Nothing in this Convention shall prevent a State, or natural or juridical persons it might represent, from pursuing a claim in the courts or administrative tribunals or agencies of a launching State. A State shall not, however, be entitled to present a claim under this Convention in respect of the same damage for which a claim is being pursued in the courts or administrative tribunals or agencies of a launching State or under another international agreement which is binding on the States concerned.

Article XII

The compensation which the launching State shall be liable to pay for damage under this Convention shall be determined in accordance with international law, and the principles of justice and equity, in order to provide such reparation in respect of the damage as will restore the person, natural or juridical, State or international organization on whose behalf the claim is presented to the condition which would have existed if the damage had not occurred.

Article XIII

Unless the claimant State and the State from which compensation is due under this Convention agree on another form of compensation, the compensation shall be paid in the currency of the claimant State or, if that State so requests, in the currency of the State from which compensation is due.

Article XIV

If no settlement of a claim is arrived at through diplomatic negotiations as provided for in Article IX, within one year from the date on which the claimant State notifies the launching State that it has submitted the documentation of its claim, the parties concerned shall establish a Claims Commission at the request of either party.

Article XV

1. The Claims Commission shall be composed of three members: one appointed by the claimant State, one appointed by the launching State and the third member, the Chairman, to be chosen by both parties jointly. Each party shall make its appointment within two months of the request for the establishment of the Claims Commission.

2. If no agreement is reached on the choice of the Chairman within four months of the request for the establishment of the Claims Commission, either party may request the Secretary-General of the United Nations to appoint the Chairman within a further period of two months.

Article XVI

1. If one of the parties does not make its appointment within the stipulated period, the Chairman shall, at the request of the other party, constitute a single-member Claims Commission.

2. Any vacancy which may arise in the Claims Commission for whatever reasons shall be filled by the same procedure adopted for the original appointment.

3. The Claims Commission shall determine its own procedure.

4. The Claims Commission shall determine the place or places where it shall sit and all other administrative matters.

5. Except in the case of decisions and awards by a single-member Commission, all decisions and awards of the Claims Commission shall be by majority vote.

Article XVII

No increase in the membership of the Claims Commission shall take place by reason of two or more claimant States or launching States being joined in any one proceeding before the Commission. The claimant States so joined shall collectively appoint one member of the Commission in the same manner and subject to the same conditions as would be the case for a single claimant State. When two or more launching States are so joined, they shall collectively appoint one member of the Commission in the same way. If the claimant States or the launching States do not make the appointment within the stipulated period, the Chairman shall constitute a single-member Commission.

Article XVIII

The Claims Commission shall decide the merits of the claim for compensation and determine the amount of compensation payable, if any.

Article XIX

1. The Commission shall act in accordance with the provisions of Article XII.

2. The decision of the Commission shall be final and binding if the parties have so agreed; otherwise the Commission shall render a final and recommendatory award, which the parties shall consider in good faith. The Commission shall state the reasons for its decision or award.

3. The Commission shall give its decision or award as promptly as possible and no later than one year from the date of its establishment unless an extension of this period is found necessary by the Commission.

4. The Commission shall make its decision or award public. It shall deliver a certified copy of its decision or award to each of the parties and to the Secretary-General of the United Nations.

Article XX

The expenses in regard to the Claims Commission shall be borne equally by the parties, unless otherwise decided by the Commission.

Article XXI

If the damage caused by a space object presents a large-scale danger to human life or seriously interferes with the living conditions of the population or the functioning of vital centres, the States Parties, and in particular the launching State, shall examine the possibility of rendering appropriate and rapid assistance to the State which has suffered the damage, when it so requests. However, nothing in this Article shall affect the rights or obligations of the States Parties under this Convention.

Article XXII

1. In this Convention, with the exception of Articles 24 to 27, references to States shall be deemed to apply to any international intergovernmental organization which conducts space activities if the organization declares its acceptance of the rights and obligations provided for in this Convention and if a majority of the States members of the organization are States Parties to this Convention and to the Treaty on Principles Governing the Activities of States in the Exploration and Use of Outer Space, including the Moon and Other Celestial Bodies.

2. States members of any such organization which are States Parties to this Convention shall take all appropriate steps to ensure that the organization makes a declaration in accordance with the preceding paragraph.

3. If an international intergovernmental organization is liable for damage by virtue of the provisions of this Convention, that organization and those of its members which are States Parties to this Convention shall be jointly and severally liable; provided, however, that:

(*a*) any claim for compensation in respect of such damage shall be first presented to the organization; and

(*b*) only where the organization has not paid, within a period of six months, any sum agreed or determined to be due as compensation for such damage, may the claimant State invoke the liability of the members which are States Parties to this Convention for the payment of that sum.

4. Any claim, pursuant to the provisions of this Convention,

for compensation in respect of damage caused to an organization which has made a declaration in accordance with paragraph 1 of this Article shall be presented by a State member of the organization which is a State Party to this Convention.

Article XXIII

1. The provisions of this Convention shall not affect other international agreements in force in so far as relations between the States parties to such agreements are concerned.
2. No provision of this Convention shall prevent States from concluding international agreements, reaffirming, supplementing or extending its provisions.

Article XXIV

1. This Convention shall be open to all States for signature. Any State which does not sign this Convention before its entry into force in accordance with paragraph 3 of this Article may accede to it at any time.
2. This Convention shall be subject to ratification by signatory States. Instruments of ratification and instruments of accession shall be deposited with the Governments of the United Kingdom of Great Britain and Northern Ireland, the Union of Soviet Socialist Republics, and the United States of America, which are hereby designated the Depositary Governments.
3. This Convention shall enter into force on the deposit of the fifth instrument of ratification.
4. For States whose instruments of ratification or accession are deposited subsequent to the entry into force of this Convention, it shall enter into force on the date of the deposit of their instruments of ratification or accession.
5. The Depositary Governments shall promptly inform all signatory and acceding States of the date of each signature, the date of deposit of each instrument of ratification of and accession to this Convention, the date of its entry into force and other notices.
6. This Convention shall be registered by the Depositary Governments pursuant to Article 102 of the Charter of the United Nations.

Article XXV

Any State Party to this Convention may propose amendments to this Convention. Amendments shall enter into force for each State Party to the Convention accepting the amendments upon their acceptance by a majority of the States Parties to the Convention and thereafter for each remaining State Party to the Convention on the date of acceptance by it.

Article XXVI

Ten years after the entry into force of this Convention, the question of the review of this Convention shall be included in the provisional agenda of the United Nations General Assembly in order to consider, in the light of past application of the Convention, whether it requires revision. However, at any time after the Convention has been in force for five years, and at the request of one-third of the States Parties to the Convention, and with the concurrence of the majority of the States Parties, a conference of the States Parties shall be convened to review this Convention.

Article XXVII

Any State Party to this Convention may give notice of its withdrawal from the Convention one year after its entry into force by written notification to the Depositary Governments. Such withdrawal shall take effect one year from the date of receipt of this notification.

Article XXVIII

This Convention, of which the English, Russian, French, Spanish and Chinese texts are equally authentic, shall be deposited in the archives of the Depositary Governments. Duly certified copies of this Convention shall be transmitted by the Depositary Governments to the Governments of the signatory and acceding States.

IN WITNESS WHEREOF the undersigned, duly authorized, have signed this Convention.

Convention on Registration of Objects launched into Outer Space (1976)

The States Parties to this Convention,

Recognizing the common interest of all mankind in furthering the use of outer space for peaceful purposes,

Recalling that the Treaty on Principles Governing the Activities of States in the Exploration and Use of Outer Space, including the Moon and Other Celestial Bodies of 27 January 1967 affirms that States shall bear international responsibility for their national activities in outer space and refers to the State on whose registry an object launched into outer space is carried,

Recalling also that the Agreement on the Rescue of Astronauts, the Return of Astronauts and the Return of Objects Launched into Outer Space of 22 April 1968 provides that a launching authority shall, upon request, furnish identifying data prior to the return of an object it has launched into outer space found beyond the territorial limits of the launching authority,

Recalling further that the Convention on International Liability for Damage Caused by Space Objects of 29 March 1972 establishes international rules and procedures concerning the liability of launching States for damage caused by their space objects,

Desiring, in the light of the Treaty of Principles Governing the Activities of States in the Exploration and Use of Outer Space, including the Moon and Other Celestial Bodies, to make provision for the national registration by launching States of space objects launched into outer space,

Desiring further that a central register of objects launched into outer space be established and maintained on a mandatory basis, by the Secretary-General of the United Nations,

Desiring also to provide for States Parties additional means and procedures to assist in the identification of space objects,

Believing, that a mandatory system of registering objects launched into outer space would, in particular, assist in their identification and would contribute to the application and development of international law governing the exploration and use of outer space,

Have agreed on the following:

Article I

For the purposes of this Convention:
a) The term 'launching State' means:
i) A State which launches or procures the launching of a space object;
ii) A State from whose territory or facility a space object is launched;
b) The term 'space object' includes component parts of a space object as well as its launch vehicle and parts thereof;
c) The term 'State of registry' means a launching State on whose registry a space object is carried in accordance with article II.

Article II

1. When a space object is launched into earth orbit or beyond, the launching State shall register the space object by means of an entry in an appropriate registry which it shall maintain. Each launching State shall inform the Secretary-General of the United Nations of the establishment of such a registry.

2. Where there are two or more launching States in respect of any such space object, they shall jointly determine which one of them shall register the object in accordance with paragraph 1 of this article, bearing in mind the provisions of article VIII of the Treaty on Principles Governing the Activities of States in the Exploration and Use of Outer Space, including the Moon and Other Celestial Bodies, and without prejudice to appropriate agreements concluded or to be concluded among the launching States on jurisdiction and control over the space object and over any personnel thereof.

3. The contents of each registry and conditions under which it is maintained shall be determined by the State of registry concerned.

Article III

1. The Secretary-General of the United Nations shall maintain a Register in which the information furnished in accordance with article IV shall be recorded.

2. There shall be full and open access to the information in this Register.

Article IV

1. Each State of registry shall furnish to the Secretary-General of the United Nations, as soon as practicable, the following information concerning each space object carried on its registry:

a) Name of launching State or States;

b) An appropriate designator of the space object of its registration number;

c) Date and territory or location of launch;

d) Basic orbital parameters, including:

i) Nodal period,

ii) Inclination,

iii) Apogee,

iv) Perigee;

e) General function of the space object.

2. Each State of registry may, from time to time, provide the Secretary-General of the United Nations with additional information concerning a space object carried on its registry.

3. Each State of registry shall notify the Secretary-General of the United Nations, to the greatest extent feasible and as soon as practicable, of space objects concerning which it has previously transmitted information, and which have been but no longer are in earth orbit.

Article V

Whenever a space object launched into earth orbit or beyond is marked with the designator or registration number referred to in article IV, paragraph 1(b), or both, the State of registry shall notify the Secretary-General of this fact when submitting the information regarding the space object in accordance with article IV. In such case, the Secretary-General of the United Nations shall record this notification in the Register.

Article VI

Where the application of the provisions of this Convention has not enabled a State Party to identify a space object which has caused damage to it or to any of its natural or juridical persons, or which may be of a hazardous or deleterious nature, other States Parties, including in particular States possessing space monitoring and tracking facilities, shall respond to the greatest extent feasible to a request by that State Party, or transmitted through the Secretary-General on its behalf, for assistance under equitable and reasonable conditions in the identification of the object. A State Party making such a request shall, to the greatest extent feasible, submit information as to the time, nature and circumstances of the events giving rise to the request. Arrangements under which such assistance shall be rendered shall be the subject of agreement between the parties concerned.

Article VII

1. In this Convention, with the exception of articles VIII to XII inclusive, references to States shall be deemed to apply to any international intergovernmental organization which conducts space activities if the organization declares its acceptance of the rights and obligations provided for in this Convention and if a majority of the States members of the organization are States Parties to this Convention and to the Treaty on Principles Governing the Activities of States in the Exploration and Use of Outer Space, including the Moon and Other Celestial Bodies.

2. States members of any such organization which are States Parties to this Convention shall take all appropriate steps to ensure that the organization makes a declaration in accordance with paragraph 1 of this article.

Article VIII

1. This Convention shall be open for signature by all States at United Nations Headquarters in New York. Any State which does not sign this Convention before its entry into force in accordance with paragraph 3 of this article may accede to it at any time.

2. This Convention shall be subject to ratification by signatory States. Instruments of ratification and instruments of accession shall be deposited with the Secretary-General of the United Nations.

3. This Convention shall enter into force among the States which have deposited instruments of ratification on the deposit of the fifth instrument with the Secretary-General of the United Nations.

4. For States whose instruments of ratification or accession are deposited subsequent to the entry into force of this Convention, it shall enter into force on the date of the deposit of their instruments of ratification or accession.

5. The Secretary-General shall promptly inform all signatory and acceding States of the date of each signature, the date of deposit of each instrument of ratification of and accession to this Convention, the date of its entry into force and other notices.

Article IX

Any State Party to this Convention may propose amendments to the Convention. Amendments shall enter into force for each State Party to the Convention accepting the amendments upon their acceptance by a majority of the States Parties to the Convention and thereafter for each remaining State Party to the Convention on the date of acceptance by it.

Article X

Ten years after the entry into force of this Convention, the question of the review of the Convention shall be included in the provisional agenda of the United Nations General Assembly in order to consider, in the light of past application of the Convention, whether it requires review. However, at any time after the Convention has been in force for five years, at the request of one third of the States Parties to the Convention and with the concurrence of the majority of the States Parties, a conference of the States Parties shall be convened to review this Convention. Such review shall take into account in particular any relevant technological development, including those relating to the identification of space objects.

Article XII

The original of this Convention, of which the Arabic, Chinese, English, French, Russian and Spanish texts are equally authentic, shall be deposited with the Secretary-General of the United Nations, who shall send certified copies thereof to all signatory and acceding States.

IN WITNESS WHEREOF the undersigned, being duly authorized thereto by their respective Governments, have signed this Convention, opened for signature at New York on January 14, 1975.

Bibliography

Baker, D., *History of Manned Space Flight* (New Cavendish Books, 1982).

Cheng, B., 'Le traité de 1967 sur l'Espace', *Journal du Droit International* (1968), 3-532.

Christol, C. A., 'Liability for Damage caused by Space Objects', 74 *American Journal of International Law* (1980), 346.

Gatland, K., *Illustrated Encyclopaedia of Space Technology* (Salamander, 1981).

Gorove, S., 'The Geosynchronous Orbit: Issues of Law and Policy', 73 *American Journal of International Law* (1979), 444.

Her Majesty's Stationery Office, *Direct Broadcasting by Satellite* (1981).

Hoyle, F., and Wickramasinghe, C., *Space Travellers: The Bringers of Life* (University College Cardiff Press, 1981).

Leive, D. M., *International Telecommunications and International Law* (Sijthoff, 1970).

McDougall, M. S., Casswell, H. D., and Vlasic, I. A., *Law and Public Order in Space* (Yale University Press, 1963).

Marsh, P., and Naraine, M., 'Satellites jostle for Space', *New Scientist* (9.6.1983).

Nicholson, I., *Sputnik to Space Shuttle* (Sidgwick, 1982).

Pelton, J. N., and Snow, M. J. (eds.), *Economic and Policy Problems in Satellite Communications* (Praeger, 1977).

Queeney, K. M., *Direct Broadcasting Satellites and the UN* (Sijthoff, 1978).

Sheffield, C., *Earthwatch* (Sidgwick and Jackson, 1981).

Smith, D., *Communication via Satellite* (Sijthoff, 1970).

US National Academy of Sciencies, *Resource Sensing from Space: Prospects for Developing Countries* (1977).

Index

Airspace,
  sovereignty over, 16
American Telephone and Telegraph
  Company, 22
Antarctica Convention (1961), 1
Anti-Ballistic Missile,
  limitation of, 117
  Treaty (1972), 111
Anti-satellite devices. *See* Weaponry.
Appropriation. *See also* Moon Agreement.
  national appropriation of area, 11,
    12, 13
  resources, 11, 12, 88-90
Arabsat (Arab Satellite Communication Organization), 46
Astronaut,
  manned flights series, 43
Astronomical observation, 91-104
Astronomy, 91

Balloon-survey, 80
BBC (British Broadcasting Corporation), 63
Black holes, 104
Bogotá Declaration 1976, 17, 87
British Telecom International, 77
British Teletext, 78
Broadcasting, 62-79, 119
  direct satellite broadcast, 65-77
  European Agreement on the Protection of Television Broadcasts
    (1961), 65, 67-68
  information services, 77-79
  Intersputnik, 45
  pirate, 64
  radio and TV, management of,
    62-65
  reception,
    community, 65
    home, 66-67
    restriction of, 65-67
  regulation of, 67
  satellite and cable transmission,
    competition between, 39,
    118-119

'spillover', 61-62
  telecommunications, regulation of,
    54
  transfrontier, 65-77
  transmission, 65
  unauthorized, 9, 31
  wrongful transmissions, 72-77

Canadian Overseas Telecommunications Corporation, 56
Caron, David D., 41
Celestial bodies. *See* Moon and other
  celestial bodies.
Civil and Political Rights Covenant, 76
Cheng, Bin, 12, 31
CNES (Centre National d'Études
  Spatiales), 82
Comets, 96, 97
Comsat (Communication Satellite Corporation), 55, 56, 58
Continental Shelf,
  Convention (1964), 7
  exploitation of, 42
Conventions,
  Antarctica, 1
  Distribution of Programme-carrying
    Signals by Satellite, 30, 67
  ESA (European Space Agency), 116
  High Seas, 7
  ICAA (International Civil Aviation
    Organization), 16, 83
  Intercosmos, 8
  International Liability for Damage
    Caused by Space Objects,
    10, 25, 29, 34, 144-153
  Law of the Sea, 4, 7, 9, 13, 41, 42,
    88, 93
  Liability of Operations of Nuclear
    Ships, 34
  Registration of Objects Launched
    into Outer Space, 28, 154-
    159
  Rescue of Astronauts and Return of
    Space Objects, 26
  Use of Broadcasting in the Cause of
    Peace, 70